GET UP AND GET MOVING

Discover Your Dreams and Purpose in Life

By Jerry Walker

www.xulonpress.com

Editing committee: Sarah Horne, Sarah Hovis, Barbara Pattee and Marsha Walker

This book is dedicated to the most precious woman this world has ever produced. Because of your gentle spirit and God-given persistence, this book has become a reality. I am forever indebted and grateful to the one who was sent to complete me —thank you Marsha.

I would also like to dedicate this book to our children and their spouses: Carlos and Cenia, Trent and Kesia, Willie, William, Jay and Tica, Raymond and Keisha, Jeff, Nikki, and last but not least Gerrard.

My purpose for writing this book is to reach all those out in this world who are hurting and to meet them where they are with the message that, "Yes you can make it. The road map to your success begins in your head." We must take control of our thoughts if we ever hope to do something different with our life because our thoughts go on to shape our attitudes, which in turn give way to our goals and how we see them through to fruition. The mind in all its intricate details will work for you or it will sabotage all your good intentions. We must be very careful what we feed into our subconscious mind.

I want this to be a book that reaches people from every socio-economic stratum and gives them the confidence and direction that is needed to sustain consistent growth. Then, I believe we as a nation will be in a better position to make this world a more desirable and safer place to raise our families.

In today's world it is obvious that we need someone we can turn to for help. Sometimes we try everything we know how to do and find that it is still not enough. In those more trying situations we need a savior; we need someone who is omniscient, omnipotent and omnipresent and knows what we're going through. We need someone with the power to orchestrate an answer to your issues and who will be there for you through thick and the thin. I believe that someone is my Jesus. He is truly the only one we can turn to for the answer to the questions we face today, tomorrow and everyday we wake up.

Table of Contents

About the Author

J erry J. Walker is an ordained minister since 1996. He has traveled to various states ministering to people, God's will for their life. He ardently believes that God has a desire for people to reach their highest potential in life.

Jerry was born and raised in Pontiac Michigan, served in the military in the early 1970's, left receiving an honorable discharge. He is a successful business owner, married for over 16 years, devoted husband, father and grandfather.

Acknowledgement

I would like to thank everyone who was instrumental in helping in every aspect of the work that was needed, proofreading, hours and hours of tedious non-stop corrections, typing, dictation, and the unity of our crew. I would just like to let all of you know that I appreciate your hard work and diligent efforts, and will be the first to humbly admit that I would never have made it without your help. Finally and most importantly, I want to thank God for giving me the ability and perseverance to see this work of art to completion.

Are you ready? Let's get moving!

Warning – Disclaimer

The purpose of this manual is to educate and entertain. The author and Publisher shall have neither liability nor responsibility to any person or entity with respect to any loss or damage caused, or alleged to have been caused, directly or indirectly, by the information contained in this book. If you do not wish to be bound by the above, you may return this book to the publisher for a full refund.

Please take note that some names of persons mentioned in this book have been changed out of respect for their privacy.

Chapter One

Start with a Positive Attitude

I cannot begin to count the number of times I have heard people say they cannot do something — "I can't do this, I can't do that." Telling themselves of things they can't do. My reply to this is "you can do what you think you can." If you continue to say or think you cannot, you will end up proving yourself right. We have been given a tool that is more complex then any system that man can create. Man - with all his wisdom and expertise cannot duplicate the human brain. Our brain is so complex that we are able to multi-task and switch emotions at the drop of a hat. No machine has emotions. That is a God-given attribute, and because it comes from God it is superior to anything that man may try to invent. We must use our head for more than just a hat rack.

You must begin your day with a regimen of positive thinking. A good way to start your day is with prayer. That will put you in a positive state of mind. No matter what your religious affiliation is, believing in a supreme being will give you something to hope in. When you start your day off in prayer you open yourself up to hope — a hope that you can look forward to a brighter day and a rosier future. Each day is an opportunity to start all over again.

No matter what yesterday was all about, whether you had trials and tribulations, you now have a new beginning. You can shake off the dust from your past and start from a new perspective. A problem might still be lurking in the horizon, but you can view it from a different angle. Time gives us the ability to mature in our reasoning of various situations. Hasty decisions can lead to error but when we have a little more time to think about it, we get a fresh batch of thoughts to filter through our mind.

You must think positive because if you continue to harbor negative thoughts, consequently you will end up with negative results. The outcome will ultimately move in the direction of the thinking process. It is as the book of Proverbs teaches, "For as he thinketh in his heart, so is he..."[1] Let's face it, we all have challenges. The issue is how effectively we deal with the challenges that come up against us, and the choices we make concerning them. Do we become victimized or do we gird ourselves up and become victorious? You can make the right decisions when it comes to things that seem to be overwhelming. You just need to think things through before proceeding. Focus on the solution and the necessary process of reaching a solution. Do not allow yourself to get mired down in the muck.

We must be ever mindful, since "the brain reacts as a servo-mechanism," [2] a heat-seeking missile, armed towards the goal and it will respond to what you feed it. You feed the mind with a lot of positive affirmations and it will go about finding ways to make it happen for you. But on the other hand, if you feed it a lot of negative influences, the mind will find a way to help you to destroy whatever you have tried to establish up to this point.

In other words the subconscious mind does not know the difference between real and imagination. Just like when you dream that a big dog is chasing you, your heart will be racing and you will break out into a sweat trying to get away, just to find that you were only dreaming. Since your subconscious mind doesn't know the difference and will respond full speed ahead, give it some positive data so you can reach a positive end. Feed the mind through meditation and affirmations of positive worthwhile sayings; feed it thoughts of substance and you will find that a lot of the obstacles that would normally be in your way will seem easier to discard, enabling you to move on to the next level in your achievement.

The mind is like a fine tuned machine. If we feed it good, positive information it will perform at its highest level. But if we allow all kinds of negative information in, it will become bogged down, and our capacity to function will be greatly diminished. Therefore we must rid ourselves of the negatives by focusing on the positive. This can be achieved through many different mediums such as books, tapes and positive associations. Positive data input will result in a more positive outlook and ultimately a better, more upbeat sense of direction.

At a conference I attended recently the speaker, and mentor, started a discussion on the brain and its capacity to learn and retain data. He talked about the mind and how we run into different people and situations that affect our attitude everyday. He called the brain "Ernie" and one of the key statements that he made was that "Ernie" would take in any information — good or bad, "Ernie" didn't care. But ultimately if it was good he would navigate to that direction and if it was bad he would be pulled in the opposite direction. The more positive information you feed the mind will help to dilute the negative.

Continuous positive input into the mind counters all the negative influences that will try to infiltrate your brain. Negative energy takes a toll on your thinking. You must guard what comes in and out of the brain, because Ernie doesn't know the difference between good or bad. He just allows it all to filter in. Beware of the dreaded negative syndrome that causes people all around us to become disconnected or detached, who stop believing in themselves. They do not believe they have the capacity to reach higher levels in life. I will be the first to tell you, it is not because of a lack of ability but because of negative thinking.

It is true that whether you think you can or think you cannot, you are right. My suggestion to you is to arm yourself with an arsenal that will propel you forward to the place you want to be. Remove all the negative thoughts and replace them with positive thoughts. Feed your mind with positive information like the text you are reading now, other self-help books and tapes. Use whatever medium that allows you to get into a positive state of mind. Keep in mind, that associating with positive minded people will help you to head down a more positive path.

How we view and treat others is crucial because it will determine what we receive in return. For every action there is a reaction. For instance, if we walk past a fellow coworker and purposely refuse to speak; refuse to be nice, your internal gyroscope will get to turning and churning. Before you know it, you might stub your toe or slam your hand in a door; something annoying happens. Why, because of your bad attitude. Subconsciously your mind knows that you are not doing the right thing by treating your fellow coworker unfairly. It feels guilty for behavior you are demonstrating and will try to compensate for your misbehavior and attempt to penalize you.

I believe that most people are brought up with the understanding of treating others right, and if given the opportunity will choose to do what is right. On many occasions in my life I have been at a crossroad, torn between doing what is right and doing what feels good. I must admit that the struggle to do the right thing is a hard one. But in the end you will appreciate taking the high road and making the right choice. I am not saying it's easy but I am saying that you will be rewarded for your stance.

I was born and raised in a Christian environment and I feel that makes it a little easier for me to discern between right and wrong, good and bad. I have an inward witness, a conviction that leads me to the right choices whenever I veer off-track. Deep down in each of us there is a little voice screaming out telling us the right choices to make. When you have the voice of conscious as your inner guide, it can make life a little less frightening. You have a barometer to help you make the right choices as to which direction you should be traveling.

There's also another voice inside of us that affects our decisions. This voice cries out "no, no, no, me, me, me, it's mine and I don't want to share it." It is the selfish person inside of us. When that side of our personality raises its ugly head we must quickly take charge and suppress it. That is an unhealthy attitude. Think of the bigger picture and deny that urge to be selfish. Be considerate of others.

Here is a scenario: you are on a busy road and you find that the backup is because a construction crew is working on the road. They have blocked the road off in some areas taking traffic down to just one lane. Of course, you are in a hurry. The car in the next lane tries to merge over. Do you speed up, blocking the person forcing them to have to wait? Or do you stop and show a bit of kindness and let them into the flow of traffic? I submit to you, even though you want to cut the driver off you will feel better if you allow them to merge into your lane. When you make the right decision instead of what may feel good at the time you will sleep better and have less stress. If you are honest and sincere and have a good attitude, you can look anyone straight in the eye without faltering. If you have a good attitude with a heart of honesty and sincerity, it will take you a long way.

Chapter Two

Overcome Obstacles

Too many times in life people tend to get the notion that somehow everyone else has been dealt a better hand. We get unsettled and begin to think that somehow the grass is greener on the other side. However, in reality the grass on the other side is filled with all types of yellow patches. What we need to do instead is water our own grass so it will turn back green. This concept applies to our jobs, home life or other relations. We can make a change in our environment by catching what we allow in our thought process. No matter how we look at things we can all come to the conclusion that life is a series of choices that we make, some good, and others not so good. But the reality is we don't always know what the outcome will be, but once the decision has been made we must be steadfast in our move forward. If in the end it was the right choice so be it. But if it turned out to be a mistake, the best we can hope for is that it didn't cause too much of a setback. Most of all, we hope that we learn a lesson from it. In life there is always a lesson to be learned.

Everyday at work I used to be confronted with two male coworkers, Paulie Smith and Herbie Hoelzeman, who thought they were born to be adversaries. The thing that I found most fascinating about Paulie and Herbie was that they were both nice guys and seemed to be well liked by their peers. But they couldn't get along. Herbie thought that Paulie was trying too hard to get others to like him. Paulie would hang around and talk with other people who worked in the area. He was known to be a "people person" who wanted to effectively communicate and get along with the people he worked with. Among other problems, Paulie had a bit of a habit invading people's space by stepping in a little too close. And let's just say Herbie was not buying what Paulie was selling. He didn't like Paulie's little habit. Herbie was a people person as well. He was a real player, the type of guy who knew the right moves to make to get what he wanted. Herbie had no problems flashing a smile, money, or whatever it took to swing people to his mode of thinking. Herbie and Paulie's personalities clashed. Everyone thought that the situation would eventually end up in a fistfight.

I, being the incurable optimist, thought the situation could be handled. I tried to resolve the conflict and bring the turmoil to an end, but Herbie wasn't having it. Herbie said to me that the very thing I was trying to do would probably end up causing a fight to breakout. It appeared that Herbie & Paulie's relationship had reached a defining moment. They had misread each other on too many levels.

Soon enough Paulie made a vow to work on a more positive outlook by thinking of creative ways to get along with Herbie. First and foremost he began to understand that he couldn't get everyone to like him all the time, and more importantly it wasn't necessary for everyone to like him. From that vantage point he began to walk with a new frame of references and was eventually able to walk in victory. Paulie and Herbie never became the best of friends. But, eventually Paulie was able to walk around without being victimized at work or without concentrating on how to outwit Herbie.

Deceitful thoughts only cause severe destruction to a person's happiness or well-being. Paulie has since departed that work place and has gone on to gainful employment with another firm. He has become a new person, consistently striving to do the right thing. He has realized that one has to be friendly in order to have friends. As for Herbie, he's continued to be Herbie. And he is a nice guy as well. However it is too bad that these two men could not find a way to put aside their differences and become friends. One has strengths that would complement the other and they could have been an asset to each other had they formed and alliance.

If you want to see results in your life the time to act is now! If you act a certain way, negative or positive behavior, eventually it will become a part of you. The subconscious mind doesn't know the difference between real and imagined. It will only gravitate to what you put in front of it continually. For example, if you imagine yourself making a free throw over and over again, in time your free throw percentage will increase. If on the other hand you see yourself being thrown off balance you will eventually see your average getting worse and worse. For your dreams and aspirations to become a reality you must first picture them in your mind.

Get a picture of what it is that you would like to achieve and allow it to become painted on the canvas of your imagination. As time goes by it will become more real to you. You will begin to do the things that will allow you to reach your goal by removing any obstacles that stand in the way of you achieving the ultimate goal. That is why it is so vital that we place good thoughts in our mind. We are ultimately in control of what we allow to enter our thoughts because in the end, we must take responsibility for where we end up. When you take your finger and start to point toward others as them being responsible for your defeats, just keep in mind that one finger points in their direction but three are pointing back at you. This means that you are responsible for your successes and your failures.

We give people far too much control over our destiny. We must come to grips with the fact that if we want something badly enough we can accomplish it. We can handle almost anything in life that we put our minds to. Napoleon Hill, in his book, *Think and Grow Rich* wrote, "Whatever the mind of man can conceive and believe it can achieve." [3] So choose carefully the road you want. What you think and believe is possible, is out there for you to get.

What holds us back from achieving what we believe we are destined to receive? Fear! We must rid ourselves of fear before we can ever move forward. The acronym for fear is *False Evidence Appearing Real*. Fear is simply anxiety over the unknown and it is up to you to recognize your fears and overcome them. I know from experience that fear may seem real at that time. It can cause more problems than you want because when you enter the fear realm, you open yourself up to all types of fear driven forces.

In order to rid yourself of the dreaded failure disease you must first see yourself overcoming whatever it is that you fear. Chop your goal down into bite-size pieces. Once you've done that, you can face the situation one step at a time toward the realization of a worthy dream or cause. Even if you are setting out to conquer the world, that's a lot of landscape to overcome. But the journey must begin with the first step. In life we all have challenges that we must face. But the key to this is to embrace the challenge and meet them head on.

You must eliminate fear from your thought process. Fear is chiefly fueled by Satan and his demonic imps. When you allow fear into your thoughts, it empowers them and they become stronger and a lot more relentless. In times of uncertainty, make a conscious decision to learn more about the situation you are facing and do not fear. Fear leads a person into making rash decisions. Learn as much as you can about the situation that you are uncertain about. The more information you have will help you to make better choices and good decision making will propel you towards your goals and aspirations on a quicker more sure footing.

The more you enhance the thought process with positive information, the more positive effect it will have on you. You can obtain information from countless literary sources and media such as books, seminars, and tapes. The information and experiences we have never go away. They are stored in our memory as images to be called when a situation develops in our life that calls for them. Even now, your mind is reacting to the information happening right this second. But since we can't get rid of it, the only thing we can hope to do is dilute it. By adding positive information the mind will gravitate towards a positive outlook, leading you to make more rational and upbeat decisions, leading to better results.

When we are prejudiced we are pre-judging, and that stems from fear of the unknown. Because I know very little about you or your situation I find myself at a disadvantage. And sometimes because of that people take the low road, as opposed to the opposite end of the spectrum where we might ask questions, get to know about the other person's situation and ultimately, find that our fears are unfounded. It's been said that "...perfect love casteth out fear..." [4] so walk in love as we have been commanded and you will be able to raise above all the petty thinking. Think bigger and better thoughts towards others. Give the other person the benefit of the doubt and you will find more times than not, he or she will turn out to be an alright person.

If you expect different results after having duplicated the same thing on a consistent basis, you can label that as being insane. That is why we must branch out to new areas. When we try new places or new dishes we will find that our horizons will expand, and our world won't be so finite. We need to allow others to come into our space to broaden our perspectives. You will see changes take place in your vast summation of knowledge by the people you meet and the books you read. So meet people and do whatever it takes so that you will continue to grow and expand your horizon.

When I learned of talk show host Oprah Winfrey's love for reading and how she was so instrumental in getting so many people to read through her book club, I got excited. People realize the value of a good book and the message that is being sent out. I come from a background of limited exposure and I feel if I can get a book published then there is no limit to where others can go if they simply put forth the effort. Background, education, training, all of these things can help propel you to where it is you're going, but they are not what determines your destiny.

Oprah Winfrey is a great example of where ambition can take you. Oprah came from meager beginnings. Her parents were unmarried teenagers. Her mother, Vernita Lee, was a housemaid, and her father, Vernon Winfrey was a coal miner. Winfrey spent her first six years living in rural poverty with her Grandmother. Oprah was taught to make education a priority, later becoming an honor student and securing a full scholarship to Tennessee State University. After much hard work, Oprah's accolades now include having been the first black female news anchor at Nashville's WLAC-TV and enjoying a hit talk show *The Oprah Winfrey Show* which has been broadcast nationally since September 8, 1986. [5]

For Oprah to overcome all the obstacles she has encountered along the way and garner enough strength and perseverance to make her dreams come true is amazing. Most people could not have gotten around her odds, shaken off the stigmatism dictated by society, and achieve the level of greatness she has obtained. Yes, most people would have tucked their tails, packed up their lunch and high tailed it to some corner. But not Oprah, she has moved on to higher heights and deeper depths. The world marvels when they see a person who has transcended all the boundaries that could have encapsulated them. In a challenging world we look to each other for inspiration. Everyday someone can gain encouragement because of her deep desire and unwillingness to give up, and for that I thank her.

In life we will always encounter things that are new to us and because they are "different" we tend to become a little apprehensive. But if you just reflect on your past achievements and how you were able to overcome other things that were new, perhaps that will give you the courage to move forward in your quest to deal with this new situation. Just remember, everything you know up to this point was new and unfamiliar to you at one time in your life. But you got past the fear and took the steps necessary to conquer whatever it was you had to deal with at the time. Problem solving is all about engaging yourself to an issue and coming up with the best resolve.

A thought for the weary could be, "Think too long, things may go wrong." Yes you should think about a situation and analyze what could possibly be the best solution to pressing problems. But once you decide upon the answer, accept it and move on. Don't sit around saying to yourself over and over about how it might have turned out had you chosen a different path. Chances are the other choices would have also worked for your situation but could have also become a hindrance to your moving into your ultimate place of destiny.

Taking the time to separate ourselves from pressing issues allow us to make a more objective observation. When we are facing trying situations it can get a little overwhelming, especially when we get bombarded with one right after another. The enemy will come in and try to convince you that there is no solution to the existing issues. But the Bible states, "For God is not the author of confusion, but of peace…" [6] So when confusion is all-around you rest assured that the enemy is on the attack and we must pull out our defensive weapons to combat the terror that the enemy is trying to paralyze us with. Just call on the righteous name, Jesus, the name that is above every name, and He will give you rest. The enemy of our soul is always lurking somewhere in the dark recesses of our mind trying to get us to submit to fear as opposed to gravitating towards faith. You can find the enemy somewhere behind, beside, up or under every fear filled episode we encounter. But you must remember, in the end only what you do for Christ will last. Christ will give you the victory, the will to win and the confidence that is needed to shake off all the torment of the enemy. Don't allow yourself to believe anything different.

The problems that affect people and the environment will take its toll on the people who are involved. You are either changing your environment or it is changing you. You must decide going into a relationship what it is you are trying to accomplish through that association. The people you communicate with in life are pivotal. One or the other will change, hopefully the more positive, goal oriented person will win out in the end. We must be very careful when we choose our friends because they can change you. Choose people who are going in the direction you are going. When you have a companion with similar interests it makes your goals a little easier to obtain. The two of you can benefit from the synergy, the dynamics of coming together to make something better.

I heard someone make a statement the other day saying, "I just don't like" this or that. What this person failed to realize is that in life there are a lot of things we will not like or feel like doing, but what does that have to do with anything? We must gird our mind and get on with the program regardless of how we feel. We cannot allow our feelings about certain situations that come up to affect the outcome. Just because a person does not feel like breathing, is that a good reason to die? We all know we must continue to breathe in breathe out on a continual basis or its going to be lights out, shut down video, movie over. When we become discontented with our circumstances the first thing to do is change your mentality. Changing your mentality does not necessarily mean changing your physical environment. Don't just pack up and leave everything behind without doing a mental examination because chances are, if a discontented person packs up and leaves Michigan and relocates to Florida you will become a discontented Floridian.

Change must come from within; we must take inventory of where we are and what it is we are trying to accomplish. Then we can begin to make some right decisions that will lead us to other right decisions. Remember success is the road trip not the final resting place; and when you continue down the path and make good decisions along the way, ultimately you will end up making a good life for yourself. Remind yourself constantly of where it is you are headed and what you would like to have accomplished by the time you reach your destination. That will help to keep your attitude in check realizing that it doesn't really matter how you feel about something, if it must be done, you must gird up your strength and get it done in spite of how you feel about it. In the end it's all relative.

That's why it is so vital that we put a gatekeeper on the negative thoughts that attempt to enter our mind. The bible says that "...for out of the abundance of the heart the mouth speaketh." [7] What we think will show itself in an outward manifestation; since we live and act in accordance to what we allow to enter the realm of our subconscious mind. We must be very diligent to guard against the negative influences. We must continue to be influenced by positive data and positive affirmations. When we are reading positive information and in association with positive people, we will become a more positive role model for others. It is imperative that we produce the positive and reduce the negative. People are watching and mimicking what you are doing and saying and if you want to have a positive effect on the ones to come behind you put out positive signals to influence them to respond in a more positive way.

We must take control of our thought process, and not allow ourselves to be victimized by the negative thoughts of others. I submit to you that they may think what they are sharing with you at the time may be important to them, but that does not negate the fact that it could be a detriment to you. You must not allow those negative images or messages to permeate your thoughts and take control of your mental faculty. Remember, you are what you think. More accurately stated would be to say, what you think on constantly will have an effect on whom or what you become. For example, if you are what you think about all the time, most men would be women. Because men are constantly thinking about women, who can have a powerful effect on the decisions they make thereby affecting the end results.

Look at statistics and allow them to be just that, a counter, and a measuring tool. Statistics in and of themselves are not bad; they are neither negative nor positive. How you will allow them to affect you, on the other hand can be negative or positive. We must gather information that pollsters put out and develop a way to beat the odds. Take the marriage statistics for example. We don't all have to be a part of the negative numbers. Be determined that you will do whatever it takes to make your relationships work and then set about doing it. Instead of looking for reasons to call it quits in the midst of the storm, why not look for the silver lining that is available? All too often we travel the road that everyone else has traveled. May I suggest to you that there is another road that may be taken, even though the road might be a bit more challenging? Of course it will have obstacles on it but I think you will find that once you start, you will be able to navigate your way through the rough terrain and eventually find yourself in greener pastures and you will find rest from your weary travels.

In the end you will find that you were able to continue because you didn't give up and throw in the towel, when everything around you was telling you to quit. God is love and when we submit ourselves to God and resist the devil, he will flee. That promise is found in James 4:7 of the Bible. Hold on to that promise and you will find that you are able to have peace in the midst of the storm. There is hope if you will just seek it. Each individual person is a planted seed and it is up to each person to discover the potential that he or she is capable of producing. We must water and nurture our seed to bring out the best that we are capable of fulfilling. When we first see ourselves we are diamonds in the rough — a lump of coal. But as we continue to be rubbed, and not always in a good way, we will begin to illuminate and our brilliance will shine through. This is why we were put here on this planet to be a light for some others to emulate, a path setter for others to follow.

Chapter Three

Believe in You

You must have confidence in your ability to succeed. If at first you don't have enough confidence in yourself, then you must lean on the arms of someone else. Our Father says to us, that He"... shall supply all your needs according to His riches in Glory by Christ Jesus." [8] And again He states, "I can do all things through Christ which strengtheneth me." [9] May I suggest that you decide to whom you give your allegiance to; and that is to lean on that higher power? My God is available to you, if you don't have any one to turn to. He states that you can, "Come unto me, all ye that labour and are heavy laden and I will give you rest. Take my yoke upon you and learn of me..." [10] God is there for you. All you have to do is trust in Him and He will be right there when you need Him.

One of the demons we are constantly fighting to keep under foot is the demon of self-destruction. The self-destruction demon is so underhanded that it creeps up at the most inopportune times. The times when you are going through a challenging situation and you must subdue, speak to the issue. As long as we keep things in their right perspective, we can expect to have victory almost every time. While we are facing the dilemma it may seem that there is no way out. We can't see the forest because the trees have gotten in our way. Such a large black cloud envelopes us. But if we focus on the bigger picture everything else will begin to line up. The biggest problem comes from solely focusing on the problem, making it more than it is. Then the problem becomes a bigger and bigger nuisance until it monopolizes every thought. If you isolate the problem and put it into bite size pieces you will be most effective at handling it.

When I started on this path, I was reminded of my buddy Glenn Hewitt who would give the shirt off his back if asked. Glenn was a cigarette smoker before recently deciding to quit. I like to call cigarette smoking, "Death on the installment plan." One of the stipulations he gave himself was that he would give it six months and after the end of six months he would try a cigarette and see how it tasted. Well of course it tasted just fine and what do you suppose followed that event? He went out and purchased a carton of cigarettes and began the trek of destruction all over again. Well we all ribbed him about his smoking habit and about 90 days later he decided to quit again.

The second time around his stipulation was, "If I gain weight, if I can't keep my weight under control, if I can't control my appetite then I will resume smoking." As the days went by we would see Glenn eating and eating and eating. To his dismay he gained 20 pounds. His statement to me was, "I quit smoking and now I can't help but eat." The demon of self-destruction doesn't care who you are or what your position is in life. If you give it an inch it will take a mile, if you give it a ride it will want to drive. So take the bull by the horns and talk positive talk. Don't allow self-defeating thoughts to drive you to the point of despair. Say things that are uplifting, that are edifying. Remember - negative in, negative out, positive data in, positive results will be achieved.

Bondage is a trap, and you might ask yourself how you allowed yourself to end up in this place. Well it wasn't an overnight thing. Bondage happens to us over a progressive time frame. We experience something in our life, and it could be pleasant or an unpleasant episode and we go back and revisit that thing in our mind until it becomes a stronghold and tries to become a part of our every thought. What we must do is recognize the thing that has us wrapped up is not good for us. Take for example living with an unforgiving heart. Something may have happened to us as a child by our parents or by another family member or friend. And as we grow older we harbor ill feelings and constantly blame whomever for what we are feeling. You were wronged and you continue to hold on to the hurt and its starts to hinder you from being the man or woman you're capable of being. At some point you have to let it go and get rid of that excess baggage.

The question which probably comes up most often is, "You expect me to just forgive them, for all they've done to me?" The answer is "Yes!" The person most affected when you walk with an unforgiving heart is you. Chances are the other party might not even be aware that you still feel this way. The other person may have long ago forgotten the incident or put in a storage closet in their mind so far back that it would take a lot of joggling to refresh their memory. The best thing for you and all the parties concerned is to shake it off. Again I say, shake it off. Let the dust fall where it will, and yes you can do it. Just determine in your mind that you're not going to allow yourself to be victimized by something or someone from your past. If you deem its necessary you can write them a letter letting them know you have forgiven them. You don't necessarily have to mail it.

The mind doesn't know the difference between real and imagined. The relief comes from writing out your feelings and allowing the person on the other end of the paper to know that you are going to start walking in forgiveness. It's as though you turn on a release valve and released all the steam that has built up over the years. See yourself in the recesses of your mind turning the valve and releasing the pressure. It will evaporate and when life happens to become too overbearing and the pressure starts to build again, go back in and repeat the procedure. It will become easier and easier each time.

At this point you're probably saying to yourself, "Come on, you make it sound so easy," and the truth of the matter is, that it really is that simple, but not that easy. It's simple because it's an A-B-C process; when approached logically the mind will allow you to realize that it works. It has worked for others and it would work for you. All it takes is for you to earnestly try and believe the outcome you are trying to achieve is available to you. Is it easy you might ask? No. Why? Because we have to first overcome all the years of negative info from others and the negative training that we've filled our psyche with. For the longest time we've sold ourselves a bill of rotten goods. We have to counter all the negatives and go forth with a fresh new start.

For too long we have sabotaged our army of men with dirty weapons and inferior equipment and asked them to go into battle against a formidable foe. The competition is not taking any prisoners. They will chew you up and spit you out unless you come to the war fully prepared, armed and ready with the intentions of winning the war. Yes you might lose a few battles, which you are probably prepared to do, but properly equipped, you will not set yourself up mentally to lose the war. So now that you have ready, the needed materials put yourself in association with like- minded people. We can start a training regimen to put you back on the road to recovery.

We must have courage, to walk in victory; when everything seems to be going wrong, we must muster up enough strength from within to stay the course. At times life with all its challenges can be a bit much. But if we are courageous at those times we will be able to persevere. Perseverance will give us the strength that is needed to continue on. While we are on our journey and we keep putting one foot in front of the other we will outlast the fear factor.

Fear will be most tormenting when we sit down on our laurels and do nothing about it. But you will soon notice by being steadfast in your endeavors those shady images will dissipate. All of the negative thinking that was trying to crowd your conscience thoughts will no longer be there and will be replaced with some powerful, "I can" thinking. There's not a lot you must do to bring about change. You just do a little everyday to change your way of thinking and the correct way will present itself.

"Death and life are in the power of the tongue..." That verse is in the book of Proverbs [11] and while the statement seems paradoxical; upon deeper examination will prove to be accurate. We will have what we say. If we wake up and say it is going to be a bad day — nothing will go right, "I just can't seem to get it together." Then you will have what you spew out of your mouth. Things will start to go awry, time will slip and before you know it, it's the end of the day and you haven't accomplished anything you set out to do. On the other hand, when you wake up with a positive affirmation that, "this will be a wonderful day and this is going to be the best day of my life, everything I put my hands to do shall prosper!" Then you will begin to see that things will come together more readily.

We should speak what it is we would like to accomplish, not what it is that we see in front of us. The Word of God says in II Corinthians 4:18 "for we look not at the things which are seen, but at the things which are not seen, for the things which are seen are temporal, but the things which are not seen are eternal." Anything that you can see can be changed and if you believe that, they will change for the better. You will have what you say. Because whatever you speak out of your mouth and believe ardently in your heart will become a self-fulfilled prophecy. So speak life and speak abundance and ultimately they will be drawn unto you. My God stated that we can have whatsoever we say and that is what you say with conviction and believe that you will receive.[12] We must believe that we will receive it when we say it.

We can't waver back and forth like a flag in the wind. Instead we must be steadfast, unmovable and always abounding in the word of the Lord. When we put his word first there is no limit to what we are able to do. The word says that, "Trust in the Lord with all thine heart; and lean not unto thine own understanding."[13] If we believe that, we will act upon that. Our God will show He is strong on behalf of all those who put their trust in Him. Remember Hebrews 11:6 states "but without faith it is impossible to please Him: for he that cometh to God must believe that He is, and that He rewards those that diligently seek Him."

When you wake up and its time to get going but you don't feel like it, get up anyhow and do anything. It's hard to feel depressed, demoralized or victimized when you're doing something. By doing something you begin to feel better and the more you do, the better you will start to feel. It's next to impossible to continue to be active in a gratifying pursuit and depressed at the same time. To be active will build your confidence and eventually, your self-confidence will be strengthened because of your success. When we are doing something, keeping busy, we feel better about ourselves and that feeling will help to build up your self-confidence.

When a person wakes up not feeling very good physically or emotionally, they should not allow those feelings to dictate what type of day they will have. Do not allow anything to get in the way of having the best day of your life. All of this is based on your state of mind. Like the theory of the glass being half empty or half full. The importance of how you look at and approach life will determine where it is that life will take you and where you will end up. If we approach life with an optimistic outlook, more opportunities will present themselves along our path. However if we walk around with the attitude that the world owes us a living, then a lot of time and talent will be wasted. We must understand that if life is to be a success then we must grab the bull by the horns and do whatever it takes to see that it comes to pass. In life you have to go and claim your success.

When it's all said and done it won't be your parents fault, it won't be the teacher or preacher's fault for what you do or do not accomplish in life. The responsibility is your own. When the sun sets on your life's journey, what will be said about the time you were given and what you were able to accomplish? I was called on the carpet with my old friend Glenn the other day. One thing I noticed is that he was not being positive or optimistic about situations in his life. I was trying to get him to see a certain point to help me to arrive at a good and fruitful end result. In other words I was trying to get him to "look on the bright side." But Glenn was pigeon holed on making his point about why I should have done things this way or that way. Its like we were in a supermarket and I was trying to go down aisle 2 while he was stuck in aisle 1. I tried to move on to aisle 3 while he got stuck again in aisle 2, and he is still stuck.

I finally said to my friend, "Glenn, its no use. No matter what I say, you're not hearing it, because your mindset is stuck somewhere else." His reply was, "What is it that you're trying to achieve?" To which I replied, "It does not matter much because as long as you are stuck in this negative state of mind we will never be on the same path." After he overcame his negative thinking he was able to constructively look at things from an optimistic perspective.

Rather than getting angry and allowing my blood to boil and temperature to rise, I decided to follow a path of thinking my son taught me.

My son Gerrard has a good theory of looking at situations. His theory is that a cool response from one will engender a cool response from the other. And on the other side of the coin, a hot response from one will result in a hot response from the other. I've learned that with patience a person can get a lot more accomplished. Instead of running around like a duck paddling under the water surface, a person should slow down and take into consideration all the different aspects of an issue. Be patient and consider the total picture, you will come to a more logical decision and at a faster rate.

Patience will help you to avoid a lot of pitfalls that you could fall into if you are not careful in your approach to getting something accomplished and this could force you to have to back up and start all over again. Take your time and gather the right information to make the right choices the first time out, it will save you from having to repeat yourself. I am reminded of a story I read a long time ago. A child was trying to get his father's attention at a time when the father was busy trying to finish up an assignment for work. The child was determined to get his dad's attention. The dad would give him a toy and then another, but to no avail.

The child would soon tire of the toys. The father finally came up with something to hold the child at bay for what he thought would be hours. He took a picture of the World and tore it into pieces, and gave it to the child saying, "By the time you put this puzzle back together I should be finished." Much to the father's surprise the child was back to him in about 10 minutes with the puzzle intact. The father's curiosity got the best of him so he asked his son, "How were you able to put the puzzle of the world back together so quickly?" The son replied, "well on the back is a picture of a man and I figured if I could just get the man together it would somehow put the world back together."

There is a lot of truth to that statement. We must work on us. When we come together in our mindset our society will come together. It's up to you. Go into the battle with the intentions to win. So on your mark, get set, and let's go!!

Chapter Four

Recognize That Success or Failure is Your Choice

Let me tell you a secret that you must discover before it's too late —in this society you can never hope to please everyone. You must respect yourself and your opinion, and not walk around trying to please everyone. Too many people go through life trying to make everyone they come in contact with happy. A people pleaser is only headed for heartbreak and despair. You can never get everyone to like you all the time no matter how hard you try. No matter how pleasing of a personality you might have or how agreeable you tend to be, everyone will not be pleased, it's not going to happen. Forget about it! Move on.

Instead, realize that you are loved and you are valuable and allow the positive attitude you display determine how others respond to you. If you are being treated like a victim, it's because you have taught others to treat you that way. Your actions and reactions to different situations dictate how you will be treated. Simply stated, you will get treated in life the way you teach others to treat you, [14] nothing more, nothing less.

When you have a definitive stance on a matter, stick with it. Soon you will start to draw some attention to your self and you will find out who your friends are. A true friend will stick with you no matter what. They will let you know when they do not agree with you and they might have a different perspective on the issue. They will allow you the right to your opinion. A friend doesn't just cut you off because they disagree with you. Realize who you are and recognize how valuable you are and others will begin to notice. Of course this does not give you the right to go around with a chip on your shoulder as if the world owes you an explanation. Just don't sell yourself short.

Do you realize that it takes more muscles to frown than it does to smile? So you must begin to realize that it takes less work to be pleasant than to be unpleasant. Don't go around spreading discord amongst people you come in contact with. Your face will draw people to you or have the opposite effect and repel them. Since we are dealing with the issue of doing what it takes to be successful in your endeavors I suggest that you put a smile on your face when you come in contact with others. No one wants to be around a grouchy, down in the mouth individual. People are attracted to positive upbeat personalities and since you are trying to be all you can be, you want to be in the presence of those people who are going in the same direction you are heading. Negatives repel, and positives attracts. So be a person that others want to be around.

Have something to bring to the table. Don't come to the table every time to take and not give, to see what's in it for you. We must strive consistently to be givers. What you have to offer will help others in ways you can't imagine. You have been brought up under a different set of circumstances and it took all of your experiences to get you where you are in life. Others can learn from the things in your life that brought you to this place. Go out, share your life and your experiences and help others to grow.

In life you will find that people fall into one of two different categories — those who are optimists and those who are pessimists, with varying degrees of either. When negative thoughts try to invade your mind you must counter them with positive affirmations. Positive thoughts will change your direction of thinking and an influx of them will put you back on the road to success. You are the gatekeeper, and that being said I submit that you must be diligent to guard your mind against negative thoughts that bombard their way into your subconscious, because once they're inside, they will tend to set up a stronghold, which will be much harder to rid yourself of.

When we are thinking positive about a situation we allow our creative juices to flow, thereby having the freedom to have thoughts come to us that are aligned with ways to make it happen. On the other hand, if we are down in the mouth and negative we block our creative flow. It goes back to a statement that was made earlier; whether we think we can or can't, we are right. So get positive, get to thinking you can and a lot of life's situations will become easier to navigate. Look for the way to make things happen, in more of life's little dramas and you will be on the road to a more fulfilling life.

A lot of people look at the situation they are in and allow it to dictate what's in store for them. Just because you find yourself at a disadvantage, at some stage in your growth process, doesn't mean that you're destined to stay there. We must consistently let the words of our mouth speak our future into existence. We will have what we consistently say out of our mouth; remember, out of the abundance of the heart the mouth speaks.

You can try to say one thing and live contrary to that and expect a different result and it's not going to happen. With constant repetition, you will start to believe that your affirmation could become a reality, only then will you begin to see them come to pass. So see it, speak it, believe it, and before long, you will muster up enough courage and persistence to have what it is you seek to obtain.

I'm reminded how in this life, two brothers can grow up with the same parents, in the same home, with identical set of circumstances and one go through the process squeaky clean with the thought that life owes him nothing. This brother approaches life with the mentality of "I'm going to give it all I got, I'm going to win at whatever I lay my hands to do," while the other brother falls into every type of destructive behavior that comes across his path. He is snared by bad decisions; he hangs out with the wrong crowd, in the wrong places, at the wrong time. He's late for work, shirks his responsibilities and just barely makes enough to support his wife, children and himself. Well since it's not in the genes, and it's not in the environment, what could be the problem? I'll give you a clue, it's his attitude.

Our attitude will determine our choices and we will reach the highest peaks or crawl around in the lowest valleys because of the choices we make. We can choose to see the glass half empty or we can see the glass half full, the choice is ours, but ultimately we will live by the decisions we make. So decide this day that you will go for the positive, more uplifting thought processes so that you can go through the door with the most opportunities.

The opportunities are there for you to take advantage of; but they don't always seem like they will be to your advantage when you first encounter them. Just like the butterfly which crawls around for a period of its life as a caterpillar, and then changes its whole persona and flies away as a beautiful gift to nature. Or you can look at the diamond, in all its brilliance and splendor once it has completed its cycle, started out as a lump of coal. So what we must do is look for those opportunities. While we are searching them out we must prepare our mindset to be ready to spot the unforeseen gifts that others walk past. Because they were either moving too fast or too slow or just didn't have the right attitude at the time the gift presented itself.

Someone asked me the other day, "Are there times you just don't feel like doing something, and if so what do you do?" And of course my response was yes. Because in this life no one always feels like doing something, whether good or bad, all the time. Sometimes the little enemy gets on your shoulder and cries, whines and complains about how it's not right, or not fair, and "Why should you be the one who always has to do a certain chore? Why can't he or she do it?" But my response to that is to do it anyway. Once you start, your attitude will change about the way you feel. Sometimes you just need to get some momentum going in the right direction and your attitude will soon follow. It's hard to stay down and depressed when you're doing something positive. So put a smile on your face even if you don't feel like smiling and you will see that eventually you will start to feel more upbeat. Remember it's a scientific fact that it takes more muscles to frown than it does to smile; so take some of that wasted energy and use it on something more constructive.

You don't have to continue being a victim because of the things that happened in your past. Instead, take a different approach to the way you deal with your past. We are creatures of habit and creatures of change. Since our lives are governed by habit why not start from this day forward to work with good habits. Since you are constantly changing, institute growth information into the process and you will begin to have positive habits take form, instead of the negative habits that you have become so accustomed to. Because of the new information going in, you will begin to see a significant change in the way you respond to outside stimuli.

The negative past will have far less influence on your present choices because you are now giving yourself a whole new set of instructions to work from. The end results will be reduced stress levels, and less tension which will wear you down and can ultimately destroy you if it goes on without being corrected. Too much pressure can bust a pipe and or your blood vessels. Too much wear and tear and can lead a person to the depths of despair and in the worst-case scenario, a stroke. Don't allow yourself to be so wound up over small details. Realize its all-small when you compare it to the cosmic universe. Keep in mind that it's all relative — relatively small when you look at the bigger picture.

Throughout this book I hope that you start to notice a pattern that is weaved into the pages. What I want you to take away with you and to allow the framework to be ingrained into your subconscious is that you can make it. It all starts with a seed planted within the recesses of your mind. We can do anything that we set our mind to do. Napoleon Hill, in his book, *Think and Grow Rich* wrote "whatever the mind of man can conceive and believe it can achieve" and that is the same premise that I bring to you today. You must get fixated on the thought that you can. Once we formulate the thought, we will develop a picture on the canvas of our imagination. And the more we work towards the realization of the worthwhile dream or imagination it will become more real to us and the way to achievement will illuminate itself and become clearer, thereby creating the roadway to its achievement. It's so vital that you get a hold of this principle, because the whole process hinges upon you planting a seed.

The book of Hebrews 11:1 in the Holy Bible states, "Now faith is the substance of things hoped for, the evidence of things not seen."

[15] Letting us know, we must plant the seed of faith in order to see it come to fruition. Until we believe to see a situation develop, we will not put forth the effort that is required to make it happen. You could never garner enough energy or momentum to go after something for which you don't believe you have a chance of ever obtaining. Something must be done with the seed. It must be planted in fertile soil for it to take root and germinate. Unless a seed is planted in the ground it will not have the ingredients that are needed to change. And in order for you to change where it is you are headed you must first come up with belief that you can achieve what it is you are trying to accomplish or where you are trying to go. Once you have settled the fact that you are capable of achieving the goal, you will be in a position to go after it. The road might have pitfalls and other road blocks. But you must have the momentum to go around, over, under or through anything that gets in the way. Don't let anything hinder you from reaching your ultimate destiny in life.

In life we must live and let live. Life is a learning process: we will get out of life what we put into it. And as we go through the process, life will get in the way, (as it always does) we must learn to keep it in perspective. People tend to exhibit all different types of personalities. They are like snowflakes with no two that are exactly alike. So when people are obstinate or obnoxious we must take that into consideration and move on with life.

Don't allow another person's shortcomings or lack of insight to ruin your day. In other words, allowing others to control the outcome of how you will live is not a path to joy, success and happiness. In traffic people will cut in front of you, but is that a reason to allow yourself to be all upset, immobilized? You're on your way to a family outing and the children are being children, they are not ready and waiting, they are any place except at the car, is that a reason to allow your day to go south? No!

Accept the fact that people are different and no one will ever do or say everything that you expect them to say on cue. If you expect that, then you will always be a victim. You must move away from that frame of mind and allow people to be themselves and to make mistakes. Allow people to set their own agendas and once you get an understanding of that you will free yourself from having a lot of stress filled days. You won't have a host of expectations for others that they cannot live up to. Expectation and attitude play a vital role in what you become or attain in life. How you view yourself and how you view others will have an effect on your decision to meet people fairly and with respect. We must view people from the perspective that they are worth something and in the long run this will help you become a better person.

Always look for the good in each person you come in contact with. After someone meets you they should walk away feeling better about themselves than they felt prior to meeting with you. You should strive to leave a deposit of hope, with each person you come in contact with. We all need hope, and the person who can go around dispensing it will be in a much better position to get out of life all that is available to him or her.

Gender doesn't hinder the results; male or female can both obtain more if they look for the good in others. And as an added bonus, you will start to feel better about yourself. A negative attitude can cause you to respond to situations that are contrary to what you are trying to achieve. Those you come in contact with will be able to sense right away if you have a negative attitude toward them. So allow the smile to permeate your whole being, get rid of the sour thinking and it will help you to see the potential within you and in others. Your ability to stay upbeat even when all around you is going crazy, will determine your capacity for achievement; and that is a pretty accurate assessment, because if you reach the pinnacle of success or the depth of despair, it will be as a result of your steadfastness.

Life will issue to you what you look for and what you have the capacity to believe, you can achieve, as Napoleon Hill wrote in his book Think and Grow Rich. With that type of thought process, he gave to the world the concept that you are able to chart your course in life. Now, long before he put it in his book, the thought process had already been given to us inside of a book. A book full of revelation and truth, that book is the Holy Bible. It tells us that if we can believe, we can have whatsoever we say. It also states that we must believe that those things that we say shall come to pass. And it goes on to say, "... he shall have whatsoever he saith." [16] We must believe that when we ask, in faith, it shall be done for us. Whatever it is that you believe God for, you must believe that you shall receive it. And be grateful for Him.

"Grateful? Why should I be grateful?" Most people walk around with a chip on their shoulder like the world owes them a living, a maid, a chauffeur or just about anything else they can think of. We should realize that in reality the world doesn't owe us a thing. We must get out there and make it happen by the sweat of our own hard work. But if someone shows us a kind gesture and does something for us we should be more grateful instead of assuming that they owe it to us.

I've seen a lot of people with talent and they allow it to go to waste, refusing to utilize their potential. They quite often look at others who have a different talent or a different set of circumstances and begin to make excuses about why the other person is able to succeed and why they cannot. What they need to do is put away all the excuses, take inventory of their own stock, and get on with their life. We don't need to continue to compare ourselves with others. If you search you will find someone who has more talent than you or who you may feel is a bit more gifted. But you will also find someone with less talent or gifts than you have, but somehow found a way to succeed in spite of their lack of talent. It's all in the way you perceive the situation.

Decide for yourself which road you are going to take. The road most people avoid is the road that could take you to higher heights and deeper depths. It is allocated to us to achieve whatever we think we can. There is a lot of room at the top, far more than at the bottom because most people don't strive to reach the top rungs of the ladder. Most things we deal with in life are just experiences that make us better able to handle other situations that develop. Each time we are successful at navigating our way through one maze, we become better able or at least more confident at dealing with the next situation that comes to challenge us. We become a little braver and we begin to think that since we have handled similar situations in the past we can borrow from our experiences and begin to take on the new challenges with an attitude that says, "I will not be defeated."

Your attitude is of utmost importance, no matter what it is you are trying to achieve. You need to check your attitude right from the beginning when embarking on any endeavor. If your attitude is right it will pave the way to success. All types of doors will open and you will be allowed to venture into those doors. Whereas, on the other end of the spectrum, the wrong attitude can close doors that at one time were opened and have now become shut in your path. My suggestion to you is to take the high road, keep a good attitude and in the end you will reach heights that you thought were impossible but have now become a reality.

No matter where you go in life you will always run into things or people or situations that challenge you in life. It may be a character that thinks he or she knows it all. Well I just happen to have one in my life, a fellow by the name of Frank. When I met Frank I didn't know how to take him. When it came to the word obnoxious I figured he wrote the book, he had the obnoxious market covered. One of his favorite sayings was, "I know everything and you know nothing." I watched his behavior and how he interacted with his spouse and children and I began to see him from a different perspective. The more I saw him with his family the more I gained respect for Frank. It was apparent that he loved his family and he was also very knowledgeable about his work. But Frank did have a good attitude on the job. Frank felt he was the most knowledgeable person on his job and so he studied to put himself in a position to meet the expectations of his customers and be successful in his work. Frank believed in himself, he had faith in knowledge, and he put action behind his faith. Frank believed he was the real McCoy and he made it happen.

The words that come from your mouth will either have a devastating or positive effect on how you live your life and the long-term outcome. It's not what goes in the mouth but what comes out that will determine your destiny in life. When we speak negative things it brings negative effects on us and it can also bring negative effects on those we are in contact with. When we speak positive things we exude a positive output that will likewise have a positive effect on those we come in contact with. Positive energy can energize people to be more creative and outgoing. Plus it helps bring a smile to your face. There is a great benefit to having a positive attitude as opposed to being a negative sour puss. When we are positive we put out vibes that attract others to us. And when we are negative we will draw that type of personality.

When we feel better we have less stress and tension. Stress and tension only wears down our resistance and allows sickness to infiltrate our immune system, weakening it and ultimately it can result in a shorter life span. Choose to avoid those negatives whenever possible, and in doing so you will be choosing to expand your life.

Because we are humans and we are in contact with such a diverse group of people, at times we will encounter road blocks. The road blocks may seem so dense that there is no way to get around them. But for every problem that we face, there is a solution. There is a way around the road block; you just have to find the way. We must look for answers to solve our problems. When we approach the situation we must keep a positive outlook. By maintaining a positive state of mind we will be more easily focused on finding the solution instead of focusing on ways it cannot be done. It is all about attitude and how you view your life.

If you refuse to accept failure you will find other opportunities available to you. Most people don't get a chance to take advantage of them because they go into a situation with blinders on; they have tunnel vision. We say a person has tunnel vision because they refuse to use their peripheral vision to see what might be lurking in the shadows. Sometimes a person has to reach outside the box or as they say "think outside the box." This type of abstract thinking could present all types of possibilities for us to succeed, in ways that were not available until you became diversified. So keep your mind like a sponge and look under the nooks and crannies for the nuggets of information that will help to propel you forward.

Chapter Five

Take Action

Never discount the counsel of those who have gone before you. No matter what situation you find yourself facing, there is always someone out there who has been through it. The wise King Solomon said, "...there is no new thing under the sun." [17] Sources like counselors, books, TV and the Internet have opened up a myriad of information that you can use to prepare. Don't allow yourself to be blindsided when going into a situation.

In the past I've had issues that I could not seem to find an answer for. I would wrestle with the thoughts for hours. Then I would force myself to think about something else, or get involved in some other activity unrelated to the problem. I might be reading a magazine article or watching a program on TV and out of nowhere, the answer almost always finds itself in the forefront of my mind. It seems when we are dead set on finding the solution to a dilemma, a wall inevitably builds up, freezes our mind, blocking out the answer. The older I've become I seem to enter that dimension a little more often. In my circle we refer to these instances as "senior moments." Don't laugh because if you stick around on this planet long enough you will have a few of these senior moments yourself. I can speak as a witness that these moments will inevitably turn into senior hours. These are the effects of aging.

I would not give up the aging process if I could. No way, I am enjoying the journey. And the journey has not always been smooth, or straight. I have had my share of ups and downs. I have had my valley experiences and my moments on the mountaintop. I have realized that it all comes down to how you view a situation. The more I live the more I appreciate the way attitude influences our life. It is not so important what other people think or say or do. It is more important how we respond to the things we hear others say about us. We cannot change the way people feel or think. We can only take what they say with a grain of salt and move on. It is the same with us all. We control our attitudes.

If you can believe that you can accomplish whatever it is you desire, you will move mountains out of your path to reach your desires. Or you can cry, "It's me, what is wrong with me?" You will not be able to overcome your own negative thinking, whichever philosophy you embrace will determine where you will end up. Change is not going to happen in a vacuum or by osmosis. We must do something with our life if we ever hope to make something happen with it. Our Creator has given us the ability to create our own future. We have the power. We can speak it into existence. Now don't get me wrong, if you just go around speaking, speaking, and speaking, you will end up with a lot of conversation, plus a whole lot of weary ears from people who will probably try to avoid you. So we must not only talk, but also put some action behind our words.

When we step out to institute change, then we will head in the right direction and change will come. Nothing comes to a dreamer except dreams, unless he does something with those thoughts. We can take thoughts and define them and organize them. But the next step is to take action. No matter what endeavor you embark upon, it all begins with your thoughts. Whether it is building a monument, buying a car, riding a train or taking a vacation, we think first then act. The idea is to imagine these things and formulate a picture. Then commit it to paper as a preliminary plan. From there reality will begin to take shape. That is how you were created. So now you can get started on becoming all you were meant to be.

A lot of people live to do the right thing, and they want to do what is right and good in the sight of their neighbor but without acknowledging God. What people sometimes fail to see is the corre-lation between doing a good deed for someone and finding that God is in the shadow. When you do good works for others, God is in the background moving things around, moving roadblocks out of your way. "Be not deceived; God is not mocked; for whatsoever a man soweth, that shall he also reap" [18] You will reap what you sow and most times it will be more than what you sow, and at times it will be when you least expect it. Therefore watch what you say if you don't want to find yourself inadvertently praying for crop failure because you sowed disharmony, distrust and a bunch of negative energy that is starting to crop up and are ready to be harvested.

The ultimate test of your actions in this situation will be your attitude. Take for example you are trying to get to work on time. You may be rushing but you are courteous enough to share the road with the other drivers and you allow a person to cut over in front of you. You will probably receive a reciprocal favor. And your reciprocal favor could come to you in any form, likely in an unexpected way. It could come by way of someone deciding they are more interested in bidding on the house down the street as opposed to the one you bid on. That is how God's favor works. You never know when you will need favor to shine in your direction but it is always on time when it does. Sow seed of harmony and reap the rewards.

Favor is a help and we all need someone that we can depend on or turn to when all else fails. Knowing that all people need help at some point, we need to strive to be that go to person for someone or some others. We never know what type of effect we have on people but we should model our lives to be an example others can look to, a willing example. When a person comes to a point in life where they feel that there is no place to turn, they should have an opportunity to come towards your lighthouse. Your lighthouse should stand as a beacon of light in this dark and dismal world. The next time you are put in a position where you can help others; do as President Kennedy said "Ask not what your country can do for you, but what you can do for your country." [19]

If you live by that creed, you will go into a new relationship seeking how you might be able to help each person that you have the privilege of meeting. By taking time out to help those you come in contact with, you will benefit from the situation also. You will broaden your borders and that will lead to growth because each person you begin to interact with will in turn broaden your horizon and open you up to learn something new. We should always be learning something new with every opportunity.

Take for example Irma Elder's story. Irma Elder is considered an automotive icon and receives much respect for her perseverance. Irma was born in Xiocotencact Mexico. She relocated to Florida with her parents at a very young age. Barely able to speak English at the time Irma studied relentlessly, met James while on vacation, love ensued and eventually they were married.

James and Irma were able to save enough money to open a new Ford franchise in 1967 and while James tended to the automotive side of the business, Irma was busy with the children, occasionally helping with the secretarial details and when time allowed, reading the financial statements. In 1983 James died suddenly which catapulted Irma into a position that was foreign to her. She was now forced to work to support her family and find a way to save for retirement. What a difference a few years can make, now Mrs. Elder is one of the most sought after speakers in the industry. She is known as the first woman to own a Ford dealership in Metro Detroit. She feels an obligation and a sincere desire to give back to the community from which she has received so much. She has been a mentor and role model to so many women in the automotive field and she cherishes the role to which she has been relegated.

Today the Elder automotive group has grown to encompass not just Elder Ford but now she has Jaguar of troy, Saab of Troy, Aston Martin of Troy, Signature Ford Lincoln Mercury Jeep of Owosso, Signature Ford of Perry, Jaguar of Tampa Florida, Aston Martin of Tampa Florida, and Volvo, Saab, and Jaguar of Lakeside stores that has finally opened. Irma Elder believes that anyone who would focus their mind on the task ahead of them and persevere, eventually they will achieve success. Success comes to those who pursue it diligently with the desire to make it happen. Irma did not have dreams of being the biggest automotive concern, when she was forced to take over the reigns, although that might come to pass, her strongest desire was to give the best service she was capable of giving.

I would say that it is phenomenal what this woman has accomplished; especially for someone who could barely speak English when she came to this country. Even though she has achieved so much, Mrs. Elder is not sitting by idly waiting for things to happen, because she realizes that if you are not progressing, then you are losing ground.

When it comes to success or failure our personalities will certainly play a role in the outcome. If we walk around with joy on the inside it will work its way to the outside and people will perceive that you are the kind of person they could enjoy being around, someone they would like to know better.

In life sometime the outcome of a situation is dependant upon who you know, not what you know. Sometime we may need someone to open a door for us to proceed through. We should be forever mindful of the way we carry ourselves when we interact with others. It is not a good idea to walk around with a frown, carrying a chip on our shoulder, with the kind of countenance that says I dare you to knock it off. Let me remind you that you will not win many friends or allies with this type of attitude and in the end it could be a contributing factor to your lack of success.

Everyone loves the happy fellow or gal who looks for the glass that is half full as opposed to the one that is half empty. It is vital for us to work on our appearance. Some people think all they have to do is get the outward adorning together and everything else will fall into place. The nice hair cut and the nice clothes will only take you so far, it will not sustain you. It may get you in the door and open up opportunities that the shabbily dressed man might not have access to. But once you have arrived at the ball how do you pick up a dance partner? Again, that is where the pleasing personality comes into play. Because we smile and have something positive to say and to look forward to, we draw others that are positive into our circle. And when you are negative you attract others who are negative, defeating your purpose. Only in math can you multiply two negatives and get a positive, not in the game called life.

When Cassius Clay started out, conquering world titles was not on his horizon, neither was being named athlete of the century. [20] All the man, who was to become Muhammad Ali, was trying to do was learn how to box so that when he found the person who took his bike he could defend himself and retrieve it.

"In 1954, Ali, who was then Cassius Clay, parked his red-and-white bike(His most prized possession) on the side of the building of the indoor fair he was about to go into. When he learned that his bicycle had been stolen, he approached a police officer named Elsby Martin, Sr. and told him that he wanted to 'whup' the thief. Martin, the coach of the Louisville city boxing program, told Ali that if he intended to 'whup' someone, he should learn to fight. The next day, Ali appeared at Louisville's Columbia Gym and began boxing lessons with Martin. Ali credits Martin with teaching him how to "float like a butterfly, sting like a bee." As an Olympic coach, Martin accompanied Ali to the Rome Olympics in 1960 where he won a gold medal in the light heavyweight division." [21]

I'm sure Ali couldn't envision at the time becoming the best heavyweight champion of all time. But if you were to examine his past you will find that he spoke his future into existence. Whenever he had a platform to speak from you would hear him spout off about how great he was. And he said it so often that he began to believe it and his actions followed his speech. Most people didn't like the fact that he was braggadocio but they had to admit that this kid from Kentucky could really fight.

We must beware of those people who come to us with those know it all, domineering personalities. More times than not, when they are acting like they are superior to everyone they are probably suffering from an inferiority complex. They don't want you to realize that deep down inside they have feelings of inadequacy. They just project the opposite side of the coin to throw people off balance and to keep people from knowing the fear they have on the inside. The way to help a person with this personality is by assuring them that you love them in spite of whatever they have been through. I trust that it will probably be a hard point to get across because they probably feel that no one could really love them if they knew the truth about who they are. But we can learn to love them anyway.

You can also help a person with a domineering personality become a better person by encouraging them to be a lighthouse. To project light and brighten someone else's day when they can. Smile, be cheerful, and say hi, do various things to display an uplifting persona. If you do these things continuously your outward actions will have a positive effect on your inward person. If you act positive long enough your life will start to reflect it. Take some forward steps and you will see improvement in other areas of your life also.

Chapter Six

Trust God in Your Pursuit

When it comes to size, in most instances, people feel the bigger the better. Take for example how most people prefer the larger sized vehicles over the smaller more compact ones. And we all know that when it comes to computers, the bigger the hard drive the better off we are. But bigger is not always the winning choice. I am reminded of a woman of small stature who sat on a bus after a long day of work and was told she had to give up her seat to a young person of another race. But the woman, being very tired, refused to give up her seat. Something inside of her rose up and said, "I refuse." And because of her willingness to stand up or in this case, sit still for what she believed in, Rosa Parks showed the world that one person can make a difference.

Just as Rosa Parks was a catalyst for change, we must work together to bring about change. Each and every person has the capability and the responsibility to initiate change. It all depends on your mind-set when a situation presents itself. When you feel you must make a difference, don't allow anyone or anything to stop you from reaching the heights of where you believe you are supposed to climb.

Where were you on 9/11? Just about everyone can remember where they were and what their mindset was on that particular day. As our eyes were riveted to the TV, some paralyzed with fear, others were not even aware of what was going on. I remember very vividly where I was. This is one of those things in life that has a way of being printed indelibly upon your memory bank to be recalled at a moments notice. Because of extenuating circumstances I was at a client's house taking care of some paper work instead of at the office where I work. When I entered my clients' home she asked me, "Have you seen the TV or heard about what is going on?" To which I replied, "No I haven't, what's going on?" She told me that the north tower of the Trade Center had just been hit and as I watched the TV the south tower became the other target. For the next few minutes we sat there numb, feeling a sense of loss and vulnerability.

Nothing like this has happened on United States soil since Pearl Harbor and for that reasons Americans may have been enjoying a false sense of security. Some of us may have thought we were a nation untouchable by these types of events. But the images on the television were a wake up call to a lot of people about the potential danger we face as citizens of this great country. The first question that came to mind was, "Why would someone fly a plane into a building killing him or herself and killing and hurting so many innocent people?" It all boils down to a person's mind-set. These hijackers were in total control of the situation. They had a mind-set of determination, albeit misdirected. They had something to prove and they were not going to be denied. But neither were the leaders and heroes that stepped in on that fateful day. They had control as well. Just look at the resolve of the firefighters, the police, and the people who rallied behind the families of the victims caught in the blast. It was a historic day by all accounts, looking at the mindset of all involved and control was a major factor.

Who was and was not in control at that time? Control is an issue that must be dealt with. We as a people will bite off our nose to spite our face, in order to show others that we have the upper hand. It's all about making a point. Do you always have control of your actions?

I have a gentleman in my sphere of influence that deserves mentioning. Let's just say he is a family friend and his name is Gerrard. Gerrard failed to get the gist of this control thing. I tried explaining it to him. I tried the rationalization technique and I tried until I was blue in the face to impart wisdom to him on this subject.

Still, I was coming back with a feeling of, "nice house nobody home!" The basic principle of what I was trying to get across to him was that you are in control whether you make a good decision or a bad one. Either way, an action will likely follow. The resulting action from a good decision may be that you will receive rewards or accolades. But the resulting action from a bad decision is normally punishment or penalty.

Gerrard could not grasp the concept that, either way, he was in control. This young man was determined to show me that because of our relationship I was in control of his actions. My statement to him was "I cannot control your physical actions or what it is you do with your body, but I will definitely control the punishment or rewards you receive for not following or obeying the rules that are set up in the house." The thing he could not grasp from our discussion is that no matter which direction he chose to travel whether upstream or downstream, he was ultimately the one who made the choice therefore rendering him the one in control and leaving him to face the consequences.

If you find that you are in this cycle, choose to make the decision to go in the right direction. Do not punish yourself. Believe that you are deserving of all the rewards that you have been missing out on. Start in the other direction, the direction of making the right choices and you will find that life is very rewarding because you quit fighting every step of the way. No one wants to take your freedom from you. Most of the time rules are put in place to guide you toward making a better decision for your future growth.

Take control of your situation. When new things come up don't be so quick to become flustered and decide to throw in the towel. Take a step back from the things that are happening and take a look at the whole picture before you make a snap decision. When we look at the whole picture we tend to make better overall decisions because stepping back allows a person to rationalize the consequences they will face. Before making a decision a person should be fully aware of what they will have to deal with and come up with a sound decision.

Taking time to analyze a situation fully will lead to a life with less stress and less headaches. Overall you can expect a healthier life absent hypertension and other ailments related to living reck-lessly and making illogical choices. People may be able to avoid some of their stresses if they would only take the time to think situations through. In this life we get so busy trying to pursue success, leave a legacy, and earn income in order to enjoy the best that life has to offer. We must realize that we do not have to stress ourselves out trying to find all the right solutions. If we take the time to think then we will realize that the solutions are in our hands. The Holy Bible tells us in Deuteronomy 8:18, "Thou shalt remember the Lord God: for it is He that giveth thee power to get wealth." In Proverbs the word tells us that God gives us the ability to come up with "... witty inventions." [22] We do not have to be victims of stress related illnesses. We just need not forget, go back to the old landmark, take the time and say thank you.

As it is now we march through life and we are so busy. We begin to think that our accomplishments are done with our own might or strength. But we are vessels of clay and we are molded into a vessel for service. We can do nothing without the goodness of the Lord and Savior Jesus Christ. We must take time to realize this fact and begin to give our God the praise and recognition that He is worthy of. I for one know that He is worthy of all the praise and honor that I can muster. He truly is an awesome God, who will not change. He will be the same tomorrow as He was today and the same next week as He was yesterday. Because of that you can learn to trust and depend on His word. He is not like man. Man might say one thing today and by tomorrow he has changed his mind, traveling down an extremely different road. That is not God. My God is an awesome God and He will be there in the good times or bad. Just look and you will find Him. The best part is that you'll eventually discover that He was there all the time and He will never leave or forsake you. That is more than any natural friend will do.

Count on God and don't allow Satan to sidetrack you with the cares of this world. Of course you will have issues, trials and struggles. You have to remember the words of our Lord and Savior, "... but be of good cheer, I have overcome the world." [23] That way you know that you have a big brother you can go to in time of stress or turmoil and he is able to guide you and strengthen you. He will walk with you along your journey and when the road becomes a little hostile and too rough to navigate, He will carry you. He is my God and He wants to be your God and He is more than able to hoist you up and carry you on His broad shoulders. He will never leave you. Imagine yourself in the midst of a trying ordeal and you find yourself on the run. But when you stop to examine the situation, you will find that it was you who left God and not the other way around. All you need to do is hold on to God's promises. You will find a way of escape, because God's promises are yea and amen. That is, He has promised that you can always depend on Him and He is faithful to perform His Word.

Chapter Seven

Set Goals

When you start something finish it. You must get into the habit of completing the cycle, and then you will begin to improve your basic self-esteem and start to feel better about yourself. Each time you start a project and fail to bring it to completion you chip away at your self-confidence. Just as, if you always do what you have always done you will always get what you have always gotten. That is why you must make a concerted effort to try new things. We must broaden our horizons but we have to be committed as well. Stick your hand out and meet new people. Go to places that you have never been before, take a chance on life's adventures and odysseys. Set goals, and then just do it.

Goal setting is one of the fundamental keys to success. You set your goals first so then later you have a barometer to measure your accomplishments. My wife and I set our goals then often along the journey we put up little reminders of the goals we have set forth. For example, we use our refrigerator to put pictures of what it is we want to achieve. Every time we go get a bite to eat, or a glass of water, we are reminded of where we are headed. Another great place to put your goals is in the bathroom. You have to visit the restroom at least once every day.

My wife puts these little notes on the bathroom mirror. One day as I was brushing my teeth, and I read one that got up under my craw. It stated, "If you are not willing to suffer the bruises of failure, chances are you won't enjoy the pleasures of having succeeded." That note stuck with me. I tried to ignore it but it kept popping back up. I thought she put the message there just for me, a subliminal sort of nudging. But no, I found out she put it there for her. But I read it and although it seemed to be directed at me, I was just able to benefit from a note she set for herself.

So I sit here this day, attesting to the fact that it was that statement that gave me the courage to step out and make this book a reality. Never under estimate the affect that something small might have on your future. My wife helped me greatly by openly posting one of her notes. By repeatedly seeing the message I continued to rehearse it day after day. The old saying goes, "practice makes perfect." But let me add to that and say "perfect practice makes perfect." And if you allow me to take that a bit further I would say that "practice makes permanent."

If you continuously repeat an action it becomes a habit. It may be a good habit like brushing your teeth when you wake in the morning or after you have completed each meal. Or it may be a bad habit, for instance a habit that is detrimental to your health like having a couple of cocktails after every meal. You begin to consistently drink everyday and one day wake up to find that you could potentially have cirrhosis of the liver and are on your way to an early grave. Posting positive messages is a good way to keep short term goals in front of you, especially if they are successful in keeping you on the right track.

Put up messages that will continuously imprint a good impression into your subconscious mind, helping to guide you in the right direction, the direction that will take you to your highest achievement. This one simple act could assure that you will end up in a better place and those whom you come in contact with will also benefit. Having positive messages around you will improve your frame of mind. And because you are in a better frame of mind and on the right track, you can have a positive impact on most social settings that you encounter.

Find something positive and put it on your mirror, or on your refrigerator, or in your car on the dashboard, any place where you are going to get repeated exposure. You will find that you will constantly be reminded of where it is you are trying to land. This will help you to develop more momentum and act in accordance to what you have a desire to achieve. Just because you sit around spouting off about what it takes to be president and what you are going to do once you get the title does not mean it will actually happen. Truth is, you will still be sitting there with the same story when you are old unless you get up and do something about it. You must put action behind your talk. You must go out and enroll in school. You must fill out applications and sit through countless job interviews. You must sometimes take positions that you feel overqualified for just to get your foot in the door.

Once you do finally get your "foot in the door" so to speak, know that there is still work to do. Hold open the door for others coming behind you. Try your best to learn and get along with constituents at your current level. Work hard and build a strong alliance which will help to propel you towards the ultimate goal. Realize that you will not get very far if you are determined to get things done without the help of others. People need one another to help achieve their goals in life. Don't try to be a one man island.

Goal setting is associated with your faith. So now that you understand the importance of building up your faith, you have to work on your belief. Faith attaches itself to belief. You know what your dreams are, now you are ready to not only pursue your dreams and aspirations; you have all the tools necessary to conquer any obstacle that comes across your path.

As you embark upon your dreams, there will be dream stealers and if you are not grounded, you will get weary along the route to attaining them. If you are not careful, you could faint and give up hope before realizing your true potential. You have to maintain belief. Belief is the stuff that allows us to become creatively alive. And faith is the dynamite that brings about change. When something gets in the way such as life challenges, difficult circumstances etc., after the dynamite has come nothing is ever the same. The situation that was first encountered will be altered making a way for you to see yourself on the path to your desired goal.

One might ask how someone can go forth after having gone through so many trials and tribulations. I can only tell you from what others have shared from their experiences that it is darkest right before the light. You have to just get up and keep going. It may first seem like an impossible feat, but I assure you that if you keep placing one foot in front of the other, you will eventually reach your goal. Remember this, "...be ye steadfast, unmovable, always abounding in the work of the Lord." [24] Keep going and don't give up because endurance plays a vital role in success. Be strong and be courageous because in the end you will succeed.

You may be saying to yourself, "Yeah it's easy for you to say this because you're not in my situation, and therefore can't understand what I'm up against." But I say to you, in this life we all have hills and mountains we must climb. And the enemy will always put obstacles in your way to try and get you to stumble and fall so that you won't reach your ultimate potential in life. But you don't have to give up, you can be victorious! We all face challenges and some of us give up along the way. Others take the bull by the horns and ride out the necessary rough spots until they get to a smooth and more level ground. The key to navigating those rough areas of your life is to see the big picture and see yourself in control of the situation.

The outlook might be grim at first view, but if you persist the view will become clearer as you proceed with your objectives. Eventually those obstacles will move out of your path or become stepping stones to the next level of your goals. If at first you don't make headway, just hang in there and keep on trying until you have overcome everything that tries to snare you and keep you from succeeding. One day you will wake up and find that you are where you set your mind to be. You will realize that all the struggles you have endured helped to make you a much stronger individual.

Another mentor once said something that was so instrumental in the fulfillment of my goal. He instructed us "to do a little something everyday". At times we would go out and try to conquer the world in one sitting and find that we have bitten off little more than we could chew. As a result we become a bit overwhelmed. However, when we would do a little something toward our goal each day, take it piece by piece in bite-sized pieces; the goal would seem to be a little more reachable.

With all my experiences I have learned to handle life as it comes. I do not try to handle next week's problems today. Deal with problems as they come. Today's problems I find to be enough. No need to tire trying to resolve a problem that has not become a problem. I handle what comes up today, and make provision for the things I may be confronted with tomorrow.

I've learned through the years that there are two wasted emotions — worry and guilt. These two emotions can come at you with a vengeance. As soon as you hear some news about something that could go wrong, your mind starts to come up with scenario after scenario about what the outcome could ultimately be. Then on the other end of the spectrum you say something to someone or you make a choice about someone or something and your mind goes into overtime about all the reasons why you should not have done it. But if you take time to reflect on either of those situations you will begin to realize that your worries and your fretting will not have any effect on the outcome.

No matter what you think about a future situation's outcome will not alter it because what is meant to be will be. Thinking and worrying about an issue all night long, losing sleep will not change the outcome. You can sit up and feel guilty about an incident for months. You may have said some things you should not have said, or did something you regret. After months of guilt you realize that you did not change the situation.

Guilt is when you have bad feelings about something that happened in the past. Worry is getting over anxious about some event that may or may not happen in the future. These two emotions, guilt and worry, are brought on by the enemy to hinder you. Guilt and worry can stop you completely from reaching your full potential, if you let it. Keep on course and do not allow yourself to be sidetracked with events or situations that you can do nothing about. Come to grips with your emotions and make a commitment to never allow yourself to be victimized. Realize your capabilities and move on.

Do the right thing all the time and you will be abundantly blessed and when you miss the mark, go and repent, start over and don't spend a lot of time beating yourself up about it. Move on with your life, you will be better off for having done so.

As you prepare to embark upon the tedious journey that I will call "your success mile," remember we are bound by time restraints. Seeing how we are finite creatures. Life as we know it is but a short period. For some it may be 30 years, some 50 and others may be given as many as 80 productive years to amass their fortune. But when you consider the total timeframe that we are up against, I must again remind you that we have but a short time to make our mark in the annals of time. And because of limitations we must be studious with the time allotted. Don't waste time fretting over things that you can do nothing about. Shake it off and get on with your life.

Every good battle plan must have a goal in mind and a strategy that eventually leads to victory. And the one that we have decided to participate in is no different. Only this war is not fought in the mountains of Afghanistan or in the jungles of Vietnam, no, this war is fought in the innermost regions of your mind.

Before you go and take on a task be prepared. Preparation will give you more confidence in whatever you've decided to take on, whether it's homework for school or a home improvement project for the house. If it's your homework and you take time to research information on the subject at hand and other related materials, when you are in class and the instructor asks a question, you will be a lot more relaxed. Because you are relaxed your creative juices will flow more readily allowing you to do a better job. Whereas, with the home improvement project, because you have taken the time to research what you need to do, you will more than likely have all the right tools to make everything go smoothly. Let's face it, when it comes to home improvement the right set of tools will take you a long way. You will make far less mistakes and your costs will be kept to a minimum because you do not have to re-cut items. You can turn the family room back over to the family in a minimal amount of time, alleviating the anxiety that could mount from having to deal with cost overruns.

When we go in prepared whatever project we endeavor to do will save us time, money, energy and a lot of frustration. We can and should count the cost, both literally and figuratively before under-taking any type of new project. Sometimes if we would just count the cost it would lead us into a different set of choices. We might decide to put it off until a later date, or upon closer inspection we might postpone making a move on the project altogether, realizing we might not have the time, skill or money to bring it to completion. This will save unneeded stress.

You will get out of life what you put into it. To the degree that where you develop your skills and talents is what you can expect to receive on your investment. If you go around all the time with your attitude in the dumps and expect to be head of the toastmasters' speakers' circuit, you've got another thought to consider. A nega-tive attitude will result in you receiving negative results. Remember you must change the focus of your thinking in order to get what it is you have a desire for. You must first and foremost believe that you can obtain the goal you have in mind. Second you must believe that you are worthy of achieving the goal. And the question might come up what does worthy have to do with anything? Well if you don't believe that you are worthy to reach your goal you will subliminally sabotage all your work. For example you will go about diligently pursuing your goals and objectives, while at the time you will be systematically sabotaging your campaign.

We must believe that we are worthy of whatever it is we are trying to pursue. We can not go by all the mistakes that cloud our past. When we see the total picture sometimes it might get a little gloomy because of our propensity to remember and rehearse all our past failures. And often we neglect to add in the accomplishments that we have achieved. When you think of your life you must draw on the good times and all that it entails, not just the bad times and all the negatives that go along with it. Once you start to draw on the good times of your life it will be a little easier to see yourself in a position out of the rut. Allow yourself to think positive instead of thinking about what you can not do.

Try to see yourself as a person who deserves the best that life has to offer. You must begin to see yourself living an opulent lifestyle, wearing the latest fashions, eating what appeals to your taste buds, driving the vehicle of your choice, and just enjoying the best that life has to offer. You are a first-class individual and there is no cause to sell yourself short. Go out and live life to its fullest, conquer everything that life has to offer and when the day is done you can say, "I have enjoyed my life."

This book, like any other good self-help book, is designed to help you look within yourself for the answer to life's most basic questions: "What is my purpose in life and how do I achieve it?" We must continue to be led by the inward voice, some call it hunches, and others call it luck of the draw. I submit to you that the still small voice that's been following you around for all of your life was given to direct your path to keep you on the road to fulfillment and off the road to perdition.

We all have choices. Choose wisely which direction you will ultimately travel. It all boils down to the choices that we make. We will live and we will perish by the choices we make. So make the right one starting here and now. One good choice was to purchase this book, which answers the question, "Do you have a desire to learn more?" Desire plus action is a win-win situation. When you act upon a thought it will produce a result. If you keep marching forward in the direction of your ultimate goal, you will find one day that you will have everything in life that you once could only dream of.

The abundant life is there for all of us. We must first believe that it is available to us, second we must believe that it is possible for us to obtain, and third we must believe that we are worthy of having it. Now the last one I mentioned is probably the hardest of the three hurdles to overcome. We look around and see some people enjoying what life has to offer. You see the larger houses, limousines, the fancy sports cars, and the designer wear on those who are in a position to buy it. And if you have read any kind of biography of the rich and famous, you will ultimately come across someone who went from nothing, some poverty stricken individual, who was able to transform their life into a life of splendor. And you can't help but ask yourself "how do I get there?"

The answer is "you get there by being persistent." This is the ingredient that fits into most situations or backgrounds to show that it is not just coincidental, but that if we would put forth the needed effort we could render the same results as the people who have gone before us. So now that we know that success is available to all who believe it; it is obtainable to all who believe it and will put forth the needed effort to obtain it. The question is "why doesn't everyone who sees and puts forth the effort, obtain the desired end result?" Because the hardest part to overcome is the part that says, "Am I worthy of the success?"

We go through life trying to obtain our desired goals but find we constantly fall short of them. Then start asking ourselves and others, "Where did I go wrong, what am I missing. I'm doing everything I know how to do but it just doesn't seem to come together, what is the problem?" My proposal to you is that when you've done all you can to bring the vision to pass, be a realist and go through the panoramic view of your mind and you might find that you do not feel that you are worthy of the success. You must deal with the mental inadequacies and work on your psyche. That is the last hurdle that must be addressed. The process is called subliminal self-destruction. That is, you tear down everything you have built up. But not on a large scale, no, some small imperceptible little thing will be there to counter all the positive work you have put into making you the success that you are capable of becoming.

As you pursue your goals you will run into obstacles that are designed to trip you up, and set you back a few degrees. You must not allow the enemy to have his way in your life. "The thief cometh not, but for to steal, and to kill, and to destroy: I am come that they might have life, and that they might have it more abundantly."[25] You must, "Submit yourselves therefore to God. Resist the devil, and he will flee from you." [26] So you must be on guard and constantly remind yourself of what God has promised. God promised to never leave you or forsake you, "For all the promises of God in him are yea and in him Amen..." [27]

You can count on God to see you through, to be there with you in the midst of the storm. Just read the testimony of a few fellows from the Old Testament named Shadrach, Meshach and Abednego about

73

their stint in the fiery furnace and they will attest to the fact that yes, God was right there with them as they went through the fire. And what He will do for one, in principle He will do for all of His many children. The Bible says "...God is no respecter of person." [28] So count it done, call on the name of Jesus and He will be right there to deliver you

There are times we get caught up in what others are saying or doing. We want to make sure that our peers accept us. We don't want to rock the boat so we go along to get along. But what you will find is that your behavior will be counter productive. You will find that you are losing ground instead of gaining mountains. You must follow your own star in order to achieve true greatness. Realize what God has for you is for you. What He has for someone else will be for them. Get your dreams out of the closet, dust them off and try them back on. You may be surprised that they still fit. Proceed to make things happen for you. Those things that were not available at one time may come together now.

Sometimes we need to put non essential projects to the side for a later date and at other times there are urgent situations we need to get on with, right now. We must look our goals and objectives squarely in the face and make the necessary changes in our thinking to bring them into the realm of the possibility. One problem we face is that we do not know exactly what we are supposed to do. We sit around and wait thinking and hoping that something is going to come along and allow us to discover our ultimate destiny in life. I don't think so!

You must act on the information that you have and go forth. In the process of you going towards your goal you will gain more knowledge and strength of purpose. As you go along, information will become available to you that probably would have never been at your disposal if you didn't physically get up and get in the game. You only need starting grace when you get into the race. You will not need finishing grace until you get to the end of the race. So get up, get moving, and you will get more insight into your purpose.

Only when we continue on our journey through the good times and bad will we get around the obstacles that are designed to slow us down and throw us off course. We have all been put on this planet to achieve a purpose and until we get around the challenges we can't begin to truly see the big picture. Once we have worked through the foliage we can see the forest and our purpose becomes clear to us and we will gain a renewed energy to stay the course. One of the good things about a sense of purpose is that it will give you more energy, propelling you in the direction you want to go. We can arrive at our destination quicker because we have a clear-cut goal. Your momentum will start to build up a steam of its own, leading you towards your purpose and destiny in life. So get a dream, a goal, and go after it. You will see how things start to line up, doors start to open up allowing you to make things happen that you didn't think was possible up to this point.

You may not always feel like doing what it is that will propel you toward your goal. But somehow you must dig deep and muster the strength of character that is needed to get the job done. You must consistently remind yourself of what it is you are trying to achieve. Once you have in mind where it is you are headed, you have more energy to move those obstacles out of your way.

Obstacles are just stumbling blocks to see if you truly believe in the thing you are saying you want to accomplish. If you believe, you will continue to push through, and if not you will just give in to the pressures of life. I say to you don't give up. You can and you will make it, if you only go forth and be too stubborn to quit.

Chapter Eight

Reach for your Goals

We the people who are striving to reach our goals must be principle driven people. May I suggest that while you are out there searching for your ultimate destiny in life, that you also seek wisdom. Wisdom is the principle thing. It will guide you down the right path enabling you to make the right decisions when you are between a rock and a hard place and tough choices must be made. It will help you to reach your full potential in life.

Wisdom will guide your thinking and show you how to apply learned knowledge. We know that it is not nearly enough to have a brain full of information without a systematic delivery or filing system to decipher all the information. In gathering the information, get an understanding of what you want to achieve, what you must do to reach your destination, and what will be the cost to obtain it. It is also good to have an idea of what are you willing to do in order to not be denied? Once you know where you are headed, you know what it will cost you to get there, and you have determination that you will not be denied, there is nothing that can stand in your way.

A friend of mine who goes by the name of Mike once had to overcome various obstacles in his life to realize his dreams. Michael was born in Nigeria in a small city called Abeokuta in the outskirts of Lagos in 1954. After completing his primary and secondary education, Mike journeyed to USA in pursuit of an advanced education.

GET UP AND GET MOVING

Michael Abiodun arrived in Detroit in 1975 as a student with a bank account totaling $500. That was by no stretch of the imagination considered financially independent.

Mike received grants and financial aid to attend the University of Detroit's school of Engineering where he graduated in 1980. Of course Mike did have some struggles along the way. While in school he was employed by GM as a Test Driver at the GM Milford Proving Ground. He graduated then moved to Daytona Beach to pursue his Masters in Aeronautical engineering which he achieved in 1982. Mike then moved back to Michigan, opened an import/export business with Taiwan and Korean exporters.

In 1986 Mike was awarded a painting contract designing paint for the auto company. He says that he was the man behind the scene. Some of the paints Michael designed included the five Viper colors and some of the Navistar's (International Harvester). During these periods, Michael designed over 3800 different automotive colors and over 8500 color formulations. The racial lines were still marred at that time so he was forced to take on a partner of a different persuasion, a Caucasian individual who was allowed to do what Mike had been trained for so many years in school to do.

Mike's first office was in the Cadillac tower in Detroit, later moving to Troy Michigan, opening a new company called Junket; which chartered planes to take people from Detroit to Atlantic City and Las Vegas for Casino gaming expeditions. He worked in that until he was hired with Chrysler in 1990 and worked with them until 1993 at which time he was hired at Ford Motor Company. Mike now lives in West Bloomfield where he still has to face blatant racism in spite of his success in the auto industry and various other endeavors. When he drives up in one of his three luxury vehicles, a Mercedes Benz, a BMW or his Jaguar, the neighbors stare wondering how he earns his living. Mike unfortunately has to endure the stereotyping from people who think he is a drug dealer because of the house he lives in and the automobiles he drive.

Nevertheless, after years of searching for his purpose Mike refused to allow anything to stop him from achieving what he was destined to accomplish. He constantly tells others how a young man who could not speak the English language fluently, 7000 miles away from his family, could come to this country and make a success of his life. Anything is possible if you do not make excuses. In order to have the desires of your heart you must be determined to make it regardless of what the outside circumstances reflect. If we can keep a positive outlook, we can change our situation. So just get up, get a dream, and see it come into fruition.

Once you have made your wish list, do a self-evaluation of the things you put on your list to see how they fit within the framework of your personality. You must give a frank and honest assessment of what your strengths and weaknesses are. Once you determine what your assets are, you can decide which of your things on the list would be best suited for you. The bottom-line is to do something. It is better to do something then find out later you were not suited for the task, than to do nothing and wonder for years and years what could have been. One of the great things about life is that in most instances we have the opportunity to make a mistake, take corrective actions and start all over again. When you keep that in mind it will help you realize that a mistake in judgment is not the end. So we can make mistakes, recalculate and get back in the race to finish our course.

The Bible teaches that we should respect others above ourselves. When you are striving to pursue a goal or an idea, consider the motivation behind your pursuit. Are you doing this for selfish reasons or selfless reasons? Consider others by taking into account how our decisions may affect those we are in contact with. Find out what we could do to make sure our plan will be equitable for everyone involved.

However, also realize that we are in a race when we are pursuing our dreams and aspirations. We must remember that. The Bible states that, "...the race is not to the swift, nor the battle to the strong..." [29] but they who endures until the end. We must continue in our quest to achieve our goals, going on with a mindset to strive for excellence in our performance. Strive to do well the first-time around so you do not waste time repeating your efforts. Leave your mark on what it is you are working to accomplish. Pay attention to details so others can see your work and want to imitate you. You want to be a role model for people looking to achieve success.

In searching for identification of purpose, we must come to grips with who we are as a person. Once identified, it will help to propel us towards what it is in life that we are destined to achieve. How can you possibly reach your full potential if you don't know who you are? Once you know your capacity to achieve, all types of possibilities become available. We can then call on all our resources and line them up to serve our highest or loftiest goals. It was William Shakespeare who said, "To thy own self be true " [30]

Success can be taken in small proportions or in massive gulps. Both are good when taken in the right quality. But it could cause problems if it is not handled properly. You have to control your momentum as you excel. Picture putting a wedge under the wheels of a train and boost the engines up to maximum thrust. You will have a train that still occupies the station. But if you take the wedge out, the train will begin to move. As it picks up momentum you can put a wall of concrete cinder blocks in its path and it will plow right through the wall. The point here is, when we begin to move, it is harder to stop a forward motion in the direction of a goal.

The human body was not set up to go full speed ahead continuously like a train. Sometimes we need to sit back and relax. Too much pressure will cause undue stress and we should keep that in mind as we strive to reach our goals. We cannot allow ourselves to get so busy and put too much pressure on ourselves. We have to take time to shut things down and just get away from it all for a while. Going full steam has its benefits but small portions allow you to have more control.

You must decide what it is you would like to achieve in life and then set out on the journey to accomplish it. If in the beginning of your quest, you are not so sure what you would like to do, make a list of things that you find interesting. The list will at least give you some ideas as to what you like. Be careful what you wish for though. Sometimes we get what we wish for and find that it was not what we had in mind.

An acronym that has always been helpful for me is A.B.M. It means **A**lways **B**e **M**oving. That is once you have decided on what it is you would like to achieve, move in the direction of your stated objective or goal. Don't allow anything or anyone to deter you from reaching that goal. The best part of the goal is that it gives you a sense of direction and a timetable to reach it. Then the action you take will give you some momentum. Of course you should periodically review your goals to make sure that you are keeping up with your schedule and staying on target. If you are ahead of schedule keep plugging away. If you are behind perhaps you can institute some stringent intermediate objectives. Do what it takes. But do not sit down and give up. Keep moving! Never give up!

When you have reached a certain level of success some people will say to you, "You are the luckiest person in the world!" But what they fail to understand is that you have done a lot of preparation to get you to the position you are in. Success does not just happen because someone wishes it to be. Success happens when you go beyond your wishes and start taking action. There really is nothing called luck. Luck happens when opportunity and preparation collide. At that juncture you will be in position to take advantage of the opportunities you have put yourself in position to receive.

To be on top, get into the habit of getting information that will propel you towards your ultimate goal. Line up your faith with your vision and go after the things you ardently desire. Even if you are not sure right now what those things are. Just do something, and then eventually your goal will crystallize for you. Do not sit idly expecting the world to knock on your door with the opportunity of a lifetime. You cannot be slothful in business and you cannot spend all your time sleeping. You will end up with unfulfilled dreams because when you awaken they will have dissipated.

Many people think that it only takes belief, but here is where I beg to differ with you. Belief will only get you so far. Belief is only one side of the coin. For example, you believe you can become president of a large corporation if you just go to school, get your degree, and do the politicking then you will eventually become president. That is only one side of a two sided coin. My premise is that after you believe this, you must still act upon your belief. This is where faith comes in. Faith is the legs that will get you out the door and moving towards your goal.

Remember my friend Glenn? On the outside Glenn appeared to be a gruff individual who did not like anything or anybody. I remember on occasions I would encounter Glenn with a situation. He seemed to come up with all types of reasons why we could not get things done. But before you get too down on Glenn, allow me to explain his motives that I later learned of.

By consistently interacting with Glenn I eventually realized that his numerous questions were to see if you had conviction about what it was you were to present to him. If you had conviction, then let's do this, but on the other hand, if not, forget it. And once I discovered this then we were able to go forward and make things happen. I'm not saying he was the easiest to convince, but once convinced he would move mountains to help you reach your goals.

Let me give you another example. Another mentor of mine, Al Hamilton, had a lot to share with the network marketing group. The group had come together for a weekend to learn about the intricate details of growing a business. Everyone waited with anticipation to hear words of wisdom from the man of the hour. As Al stood at the podium, dressed for success in his Bill Blass suit you could not help but admire him and where he came from.

Al was raised in Alabama by his grandmother. One thing she instilled in him was the idea that he could do anything anyone else could do. Years later when Al was working for one of the major automotive companies in Michigan he found himself in need of a more lucrative position to support himself and his new growing family. He felt he could do better so he applied for a promotion into a skilled trade position. Others tried to convince Al that it was just a waste of time.

Opportunity does not always appear as an opportunity when it shows up. Al was in a situation in which he would have to take a pay cut to go to school, and he would have to take additional classes. But Al was willing to do whatever was necessary to realize a better life for his family. He took on the role and immediately started working towards building a brighter future. Soon Al would meet the guy who would change his direction allowing him to enjoy true freedom.

Again, opportunity does not always appear plainly. His new opportunity showed up in a veiled box. One of Al sons fell ill and needed constant attention. His wife Fran's job would not allow her to take time off to tend to their son. Adversity will either grow you or defeat you. Al and his wife Fran were forced to make a decision. Fortunately they had their vertical alignment lined up right: God, family, then work. Plus they had already decided they had an opportunity that could catapult them into the ranks of the rich and famous.

They set a goal where they would be financially stable, and that would enable Fran, (a little dynamo) to leave her good job to come and be a stay at home mom. Fran was able to give her son the attention that was needed at a critical time in his life. This giant of a man with an obscure background now sits and jet sets with the rich and famous.

Al kept his eyes on the prize and was determined to make it happen for him and his family. He did not take no for an answer. Al tells us if you put some elbow grease and some positive thinking together. You can accomplish whatever in life you put your mind to. And I can follow leadership like this because the two of them not only talk the talk but Al and Fran walk the walk.

When you find that you are not where you would like to be, all you have to do is take corrective steps to change your direction. The thing about goals is that they keep you on track. You don't have to start all over again from the beginning. No, you go from where you are and institute the corrective actions that will put you on course.

Chapter Nine

Find Happiness in the Journey

I have noticed that people often attempt to buy self-esteem with toys and baubles and are never successful at receiving satisfaction from it. They buy the Gucci bags and Gucci glasses, Corvettes and BMW's, only to find they still don't feel good about themselves. They measure themselves by their material possessions. But what they fail to realize is that it is the inner person that needs fostering.

People eventually realize that they will never feel good about themselves until they grasp the notion that they must love themselves despite their faults and their material possessions. I refer to these types as "people pleasers," and they really have a hard time until they come to the realization that you can never please everyone. No matter who you are or what level you are on or how big your fortune is, someone will be unimpressed. Once this is recognized then a person can move forward working on themselves, boosting their self-esteem. Self worth can be improved. Doing something positive or constructive helps.

Each time you complete a goal you set out to achieve it builds upon your basic self-esteem. Take your eyes off of others and get them locked in on you, and the things in life you want to accomplish. Now do not misunderstand what I am saying. I am not talking about being selfish or self absorbed, concerned only with you, you, you. I am talking about having a healthy love affair with the person who travels with you everywhere you go. You must strive to like self first. And you can do that without neglecting those that are significant in your life.

Recognize that we are put here for a purpose and the idea is to go about finding out what that purpose is. "What is it that God has ordained me to do?" Or if you have a lifetime partner the question is "what is it that God has ordained us to do?" Once you get busy working toward your purpose or even searching for it you will find happiness. Some people don't find happiness until they reach the end and get resolve, once they can declare an accomplishment. But happiness can and should be discovered in your journey towards finding your lifetime goal or objective. If you look only at the end result you may be missing the point.

The pursuit of obtaining your goals will bring you happiness. When you are trying to achieve something you are learning, working through your issues, enjoying life in the process. If you just wait to the end result you may feel a sense of letdown. We as a people get so caught up in our work that we don't take time to smell the roses and enjoy the moment. In your pursuit of happiness take time to enjoy life as it is. Slow down, enjoy the day and take a load off, you will begin to relax and life will become a little less stressful and hopefully a lot more enjoyable.

You will see such a difference in your life after you start making some progress toward finding your purpose. You will want to share with others your secret to finding happiness. But do not expect others to live exactly as you suggest. Making plans for others will ultimately make you frustrated and open you up to a lot of anxiety. No one can control the people around them. People are people, and because we are motivated from within, we will only witness stress and heartbreak when we attempt to motivate others with outside stimuli. Most time it just doesn't work.

What we can do is enlighten others. Tell them of the rewards associated with doing something worthwhile for themselves. If you have a desire you can really work with them by giving them incentives for reaching certain milestones towards there goals. But it is still up to them. Our motivation must come from within. We must decide what it is we want and what type of effort we are willing to put into bringing about the desired results.

Advancement is a good thing. Everybody wants to be the top achiever at one point in their lives. I don't see anything wrong with having big dreams because it drives people towards advancement. It is a great thing to strive for higher heights and going for what we know we are capable of achieving. You should want to make the most out of your life. However what we cannot do and should not do is crush the competition on the way up. Just remember those same people you step on to get to the top you may need to buffer your fall on the way down.

Esteem your fellowman, knowing we can reach our goals and still treat others with dignity. How we view our neighbor will determine how we treat them. If we have the view that others are just a stone in the road or just another cog in the wheel that turns, then the only worth we loan to these people is someone to be used to obtain our goal.

We must realize that this person is someone who has value, and we should take time and give this person a chance to develop the skills and talents that may be lying dormant. Who knows? Perhaps you were put in that person's life to cultivate hidden talents. When that person wants their talent to be cultivated, the teacher will appear.

As we travel down the path towards our goal, sometimes things will get a little rough, the road ahead will seem to be a bit treacherous but we must continue in spite of what we see ahead of us. Opportunity has a way of disguising itself. Most of the time it's not going to present itself as something nice and easy, on the contrary, it will probably appear as hard work with no apparent successful end in sight.

You must be steadfast and unmovable and call on your inner reserves and when they run out you must go to a more creative source. You always have a helper that is available to you but all too often people wait until they are out on the limb before calling on Him and allowing Him to walk beside them helping to sustain a steady path.

An example of steadfastness is Leonard Darden. Leonard was born in 1955, has been married for 11 years to a wonderful supportive wife who he declares his undying love. She has been through the thick and thin with him. He was schooled in the Detroit area, obtaining his engineering degree and secured employment with Focus Hope Training Center as an assistant manager and instructor.

With all that said the thing that I find most amazing about Leonard is his zeal for life in spite of the enemy coming against his body in 1995 with throat cancer. He endured radiation treatment until 1996; then in 2002 he was diagnosed with pre-leukemia which he was last treated for in 2005.

In the midst of all this, every time I would see Leonard he would respond with exuberance, "God is good and He is going to deliver me out of this situation." Long before the victory was manifested in the natural, he was confident that his God was able and not only able He would deliver him. Leonard reminded me of the three Hebrew boys who told King Nebuchadnezzar that their God was able to deliver them from his mandate.

Leonard refused to feel sorry for himself and walk around with his countenance down. He knew to whom he put his trust in and God rewarded him for his faithfulness and his unwillingness to bend, when things were not going right in his body.

This man was also addicted to drugs, from the time he was 15 until he was 34. His motto was whatever goes when the whistle blows. In 1987 he got clean with God's help, nothing else had worked and since God has delivered him, he has never turned back.

That is why Leonard is sold out to the Lord of Lords and the King of Kings. And the question is why everyone can't trust in this wonderful God that is available to all who would call on Him.

You can do all things that you put your minds to do. When you get down and begin to feel that you can't go on any longer at the pace that you have been traveling, let go and let God take over. Remember, God will supply all your needs according to his riches in glory by Christ Jesus. [31] Once you get that together inside your heart, it will help to make life's journey a little easier to navigate. The question might come up, "How can I get God to come and work beside me?" Well that is a question that begs for an answer. In the

Bible, (which I've heard others use the acronym as **B**asic **I**nstruction **B**efore **L**eaving **E**arth), the book of Revelation says, "Behold I stand at the door and knock: if any man hear my voice, and open the door, I will come in to him, and will sup with him, and he with me." [32] So there you have it, an open invitation to have fellowship with the Lord God Almighty.

He came to the earth as a man and lived on the earth for 33 years, died and sent back a companion for you called the Holy Spirit. And the Holy Spirit comes to dwell inside of you, and to walk with you through any and every situation that may develop. And the Word says, "Surely goodness and mercy shall follow me all the days my life…" [33] so you can rest assured that once you have accepted our Lord and Savior in your life He will abide with you forever.

To pursue your dreams and aspirations you must be focused and stay on task. There are a lot of situations out here that are vying for your attention and a lot of those things are designed to shipwreck your dreams. For if your desires are to obtain a new home, and yet your constant thoughts are on going to the gambling casinos, you have taken yourself off task and have decided to replace your ultimate goal with a temporary fix that could turn into a permanent nightmare. Do not lose focus of your ultimate goal.

Make small strides toward your ambitions each day. When you get into the practice of doing something towards your goals everyday it will become a habit, and that is how you replace bad habits. You repeat good behavior until the bad habit is no longer there. And the negatives that you thought were so strong and overpowering will lose their appeal. Negatives become more powerful when they are left unchecked, they will grow and multiply.

However the same theory applies to positive behavior. Like for instance those positive messages that you say to yourself. After you consistently repeat what you want and where it is you are headed it will eventually create its own momentum and build up steam. Then you will find that it has become easier to look for and notice more positive situations.

We do reach points in life where we have to make important decisions. Life has a way of changing whether we are ready or not. But what do you do when you have no idea which direction you should head? You may have already faced such instances on more than one occasion. How do you handle it? Or do you handle it at all?

Have you ever been at the crossroad of a career change and things just seem to happen? One job might bring about some drastic changes that do not fit into your lifestyle or do not agree with your schedule. Then something new comes along and the new job has the perfect schedule, friendly atmosphere, and weekends off. But once you get there your spirit is still restless. That might be an indication that you did not make the right choice.

A different opportunity may be near. This other opportunity comes into play and off the bat it might have some things out of place. Say the boss is a bit demanding or brash. And the pay does not seem to be much better. But you accept this new opportunity and unexplainably you feel peace on the inside. That is a subtle indication that you have made a good decision. You probably gravitated toward this position because it was the one for you.

You must work from your inner signals. This is the voice of your conscious. For when that inner signal is at rest that is probably the right choice. All too often you ignore that small voice trying to lead and direct you into the right path. So listen and you will be led down the right path.

The bottom line is, sometimes you must throw all caution to the wind and follow your heart. When you follow your heart and not the dictates of others, it will lead you down the path to all that life has in-store for you. On the other hand when you follow the crowd, they will try to tell you all the reasons why things will not work for you. They may even give examples of all the people who have tried it in the past and failed. That is why you must listen to your own heart and not the naysayer.

We all started off in life headed in the same direction and that is upward. Somewhere along the way people get sidetracked and become misdirected. Statistics show that out of 100 people, one of them will become rich, five of them will become financially independent, and the rest will fritter away. I expect that it is not due to lack of ability. Most people have the ability to reach higher heights but somehow in the process of living allow negative situations to sidetrack them. Do not allow negative influences to derail you from achieving your hopes and dreams.

You must strive hard to maintain a watchful eye on your thoughts and be vigilant at ejecting those thoughts that are contrary to your objective. In order to achieve true success we must recognize that we are solely responsible for where we are in life. Along the way you will have people who will influence you to go in this direction or the other. Ultimately you are the one who make the final decision as to which direction to proceed in. Just as you have control over whether or not you will be successful, by the same token you shoulder the responsibility of your inability to reach your true desires.

You want to preserve your potential for success. That is why it is so important to protect your eyes and ear gates. Do not allow just anything to enter in. The enemy would like to bombard you with all kinds of negative information to shipwreck your faith. But you can not allow that to happen.

What you have to do is get to know God. The Bible tells us in Proverbs that "The fear of the Lord is the beginning of wisdom...." [34] It is vital that you take the time from your busy schedule to seek God and learn of Him. He will give you the key to wisdom and spiritual understanding. No man can teach you everything you need to know. You don't need any man teach you but the anointing you have received of Him which is the Holy Ghost. [35] He will be your teacher and your guide when you travel on roads that are unfamiliar. Our God will show you how to navigate through the storms to the peaceful shores.

We will succeed or we will fail by the choices we make. Life is a series of choices. Which door you enter will be largely determined by the training you have had up to this point. Keep in mind that whether you have had a lot of positive re-enforcement or negative re-enforcement in your past, this day is the beginning of a new existence for you. Whatever you do from here on out will determine your level of achievement.

You can make it happen, no matter what the dream or goal. It all starts within the framework of your mind. You must believe that the possibility exists, or you will never take those first fear filled steps forward. After you have determined that it can be done, you need the confidence to take the next steps. Then you take another and another until you have accomplished what you have always wanted to achieve.

The old maxim, how do you eat an elephant? You eat it one bite at a time. How do you overcome fear? You tackle it one baby step at a time. Once you are successful at step one, you allow that person who has had a taste of success to move on to the next step. Then when you succeed at step two, you allow that person to go to the next step, then before you know it you have overcome the fear and trepidation that was holding you back.

Chapter Ten

Don't Get Stuck

W hat I have noticed about most people is that they will get all excited about a new idea, dream, or goal that comes their way. They get involved and throw all caution to the wind. Things may become a little complicated or obstacles get in the way. Then there is a reversal in the amount of enthusiasm that is spent in the direction of their goal. Before long, if they are not committed they are off and running to some new project. Out with the old and in with the new.

"But" and I must admit it is a big "but." If you can garner some strength and renewed vigor you can redevelop your enthusiasm for the original project. Go to God for that strength. He will rejuvenate you and help you achieve completion. Every time you bring a project to completion it will have a triumphant effect on you. It will help you feel better about yourself and your basic self-esteem will increase.

When you first start on your journey to achieve your dreams it may appear that you have all the time in the world to accomplish the task. But it seems like once you attach a goal to it, you have placed a box around it with a clock inside. Before, time didn't matter but now you have a deadline. Now that you have placed parameters around when the vision is to be accomplished you can work towards it. You know exactly when you should arrive at the desired destination.

Having a timeline will allow you to know if you are ahead of schedule and have time to spare, or have fallen behind prompting you to eliminate those things that will waste your time. Prevent emergency time constraints by first concentrating on the essential things that are needed to accomplish your main objective. And be persistent in your efforts to bring to pass whatever you have chosen to do. When you are persistent, doors will open up. Doors that are closed to you in the beginning will ultimately start to open. The reward for being persistent is that you will start to feel better about yourself and your self-esteem will be greatly enhanced.

Take into consideration how water flows. Water will flow up stream or it will flow down stream. The thing about water is that it is not about to allow anything to stop its flow. When it runs into an obstacle it finds a way to flow through it, over it, under it or around it. Notice I did not say anything about it stopping.

What I am saying to you is that when you are persistent a path will present itself to you. You will find ways to proceed and reach your goals and objectives. When others try to tell you it can not be done, think of all the people who made it in spite of the circumstances that surrounded them. Draw on their courage and tenacity until you can muster up your own.

Smile big from the inside out. You will feel better about the situation and the people you come in contact with. They will think of you as a more upbeat person. A smile can change the way others react to you, paving the way for good relationships with people who may be able to help you along the way.

When our nation mourned the passing of former President Ronald Reagan we could not help but see a person who was larger than life, a seemingly perfect specimen of a man. But a closer look into his past reveals an individual who had an alcoholic father that was often absent from his life. Reagan was a man who started out in a modest environment doing normal activities such as working as a lifeguard. Although he had loftier dreams, one of which was of becoming an actor. Before long he was able to accomplish that goal by becoming one of the Hollywood's leading men. After acting Reagan turned his attention towards politics and served two terms as the governor of California prior to serving two terms in the White

House. Reagan found a way to work around his obstacles to become a success and so can you!

When you find yourself deadlocked about a situation you have been working on and you find you do not know which way to turn, just do something. Do anything, and that will start the momentum to propel you forward. Just lying there or sitting there will not improve your situation. The mere fact of you getting up and doing anything will make you feel better and give you a more positive outlook. Take charge and go for it.

Sometimes we run into roadblocks in our life and in the way we are traveling. Don't just sit at the cross road, hoping that somehow or some way a road will open up for you. Make a way for yourself. If you just sit there and just ponder on your ideas nothing will happen. That is not what you do. In instances where you reach a dead end you should take a detour and look for an alternative route in which to travel.

Much like the physical roadways that we travel on, when you are at an impasse you may have to feel your way through. Know that there has to be another way and find it. Don't just stop. We do not have to allow ourselves to get shut down. Take action. If one way does not work we use our creativity to try other methods. Then when everything that you have tried is not working, take a break. Give yourself a little time to let the engines cool down and then after having taken a break, you can get right back at it. You will begin to see that in most cases you will have gained a new perspective on the situation and now you attack the situation from a different angle.

We must be proactive and not just reactive. We can go out and make things happen and create our own destiny. Or we can wait for things to happen and then respond to the things that are going on. Being reactive could result in someone else dictating what is right for you. I know you want to experience everything you want for your life. Most people want to have a life full of love, joy, peace and prosperity just to name a few things. And these things are out there for those who will go out and make it happen. You have every opportunity to accomplish your life's ambition which will enable you to enjoy your life with those people who are depending on you. Go forth and make things happen.

No doubt we are all faced with hard situations. No one is immune from having to travel down that road. But when you run into difficult trying circumstances you feel you can not deal with, call on your inner strength. It is there, it might be hidden under a layer of outdated ideals that had their place at one time. But rest assured that with a little practice we can build up our ability to say yes to our will and also be capable of saying no when appropriate.

The flesh wants to have its way but we must train our flesh to submit to the will. We do this by putting our body under subjection. We start with little things and work our way to the larger more important issues. Do not go after the biggest issues first because along the way you are bound to become discouraged if you do not witness success right away. However, if you train yourself with the small successes your mind will know that you are truly able to subject your body to your will.

The key to winning any type of permanent change is through establishing new habits. We are all creatures of habit. Since you are going to habitually do something anyhow, why not do something that is constructive, healthy and in your best interest. Whether good or bad you are going to develop habits. I say just adopt good things to practice. When your good practices become permanent you will be better off.

As my mentor George Logan worked his way through the crowd you could sense the excitement level was starting to build. As he made his way to the stage the anticipation was at an all-time high. What new information would he impart today? As George opens his talk, he acknowledges the crowd and introduces himself as "Mr. Excitement," and the crowd goes crazy. So many stories had been told. Mr. Excitement's reputation preceded him. This man is in his seventies and has more energy than a twenty year old. He has caused a lot of men half his age to sit back and take note.

Mr. Excitement worked for one of the automotive supply companies. So many people look for reasons why a thing will not work, but not George. He did not allow the fact that he was a minority stop him from reaching his goal. With a lot of hard work George was promoted to superintendent. He continued to work hard for his employer and the rewards came in the shape of a company car, expense account, and a trip to the spa with some racquetball court time.

Eventually a new owner came on the scene and the winds of change started to rear its ugly head. George figured he had better think about changing with the tide and to his amazement someone offered him the opportunity to earn some extra money in a network marketing business. Always the optimist, George felt it could not hurt to try it. After taking a look at what his co-worker had to offer, George decided to take a chance and see what the outcome would be. He reasoned that whatever he earned would be extra, and took the plunge.

To his amazement people were interested in what he had to offer. He began to realize that he could have a solid impact on the lives of the people he came in contact with. When his company offered him an early out he took it. George then jumped at the opportunity to make it on his own and his marketing business flourished. He interacts with a host of people from the bottom of the social strata to the top of the economic chain. Mr. Excitement is traveling across the country bringing hope to all who will take the time to hear what he has to share and he is doing a phenomenal job of it.

Within the framework of this life, if there is ever going to be a change in your environment or circumstance you must be the catalyst for change. You must step up to the plate, take a stand and let your voice be heard. Whether internal or external you must be the person who orchestrates the process for change. I suggest that you focus on the internal first. Pay close attention to what you allow to filter into your thinking process and make a decision now to be consciously aware of what you allow in.

When your thinking goes south, or gets negative, make a solid effort to correct it right away. Do not just sit there and make excuses for why you're thinking negative, get something positive to focus on. If you need outside stimulus which at first might be necessary, get a tape, book or TV program that is positive to help yourself out. Eventually, you will be able to recall positive information that has already been deposited. Once this becomes regimented, you will find that it is easier to flip the switch from the negative train of thought to a more positive way of looking at things.

Keep in mind, if change is going to occur you must be the catalyst or the instrumentation that will facilitate the change. In order to change from one format to another, we must change our basic habits. Change is not a bad word even though people tend to stay with the familiar. Habit is not a bad word either. Truth is, we are all people of habit and our life really consists of a series of habits that we have picked up along the way. Realize that in order to change a habit you must do some things differently to change or modify that behavior. Change will not come automatically. You must force the change.

Let me rationalize this for you. If life is a series of habits and if you want some aspect of your life to be different or changed, then you must change your habits. You must determine if your habit will take you closer to where you have decided to go in life, or take you away from a predetermined goal. It has already been established that goal setting is a good habit to get into. The goal is just an objective of where you want to go. Put something out there to reach toward and give yourself a timetable to reach it. Check periodically to see if you are on track to reach or obtain the desired results.

Take a look at the following timeline. Do you think most people would look at it and consider the person a failure or a success? Most would probably say he was a failure because of the many times he was defeated, but if you look past the defeats you will see a perfect example of how persistence pays off. [36]

Year	Event
1832	Lost job, defeated for state legislature
1833	Failed in business
1835	Sweetheart died
1836	Had a nervous breakdown
1838	Defeated for speaker of the house
1843	Defeated for nomination for Congress
1848	Lost re-nomination
1849	Rejected for land officer
1854	Defeated for U.S. Senate
1856	Defeated for nomination for Vice-President

| 1858 | Defeated again for U.S. Senate |
| 1860 | Elected President of the United States |

These actions are examples of persistence displayed by our 16th President, Abraham Lincoln. He didn't allow setbacks to stop him from achieving his ultimate goal. When he went into something and it didn't work out he didn't tuck his tail, whimper away and quit, no! What he did was gird up the resources of his mind, told himself that he could make it in spite of the situation at hand and went for the next goal.

You can tell by reading the list, success did not come easy or without its hardship. But ultimately, when it came it came in abundance. And the reward of victory overshadowed every trying circumstance, every setback. In the end Abraham Lincoln was known as one of the greatest presidents that was ever elected. So revisit your dreams, put them out in front of you and go for it. One thing is for certain, you will never be all that you could be unless you try. Nothing beats failure except when we try. The key is that you cannot fail as long as you try something new. The mere fact, that you're trying instead of giving up shows that you are a winner.

The defeatist attitude is, "I've tried and it didn't work out, so what is the use, I may as well give up." There is a whole world of new vistas that you can go out and conquer. Do not ever be like the defeatist. Mimic the optimist, and go for it. You can never make it around the bases unless you take off and head for home plate. Once you place the goal in your mind all you have to do is continue to apply yourself until you reach the desired results. On the way you may become a little side tracked and get thrown off target. But once you realize that you are off target just correct yourself and straighten out your direction.

Do not beat yourself up. Anyone can get off track, it happens. Just get back in the race. The key is not to wallow in self-pity telling yourself that you will never accomplish your goal. Tell yourself you will.

Some people feel that if they come out of a dysfunctional family environment that will dictate how far they will be able to go or what they will be able to achieve in life. I would like to share with you a truth that can give you a new set of hope. Your background or present living situation has nothing to do with your growth potential. No matter what environment or the circumstances you are now facing, if you look around and do a little research you will find someone who is a success in life who came out of a similar set of circumstances. Where you begin has nothing to do with where you will end.

Know that you can always go beyond. There are no limits to where you are capable of going. The true barometer of what lies ahead for you is what your mind is tuned into. Are you an optimist or a pessimist? Do you see the glass half full or the other end of the spectrum, half empty? That will be more important in the long run. Be consistent in your endeavor to achieve your goals and objectives and one day in the not to distant future you will see them start to materialize. You will see things start to take form on the horizon.

Chapter Eleven

Open Your Heart to Change

We can always overcome shortcomings if we would just put forth a concerted effort. With time the most stubborn problems will erode and melt away. Continue to be steadfast and work towards the building of your dreams and you will see them continue to get closer and closer until they become a reality. You will succeed if you persist. Persistence pays off. It is proven to work if we will only stay steadfast.

It is so important that you begin to put forth effort and continue prodding along inch by slow inch and you will begin to see changes. Even your most stubborn stain will give way when you work at it day by day. The key to bringing about change is to be aware of your shortcomings. If you know that you have a deficit in some area of your life don't give in or give up. Do whatever is necessary to put that part of your life in order.

If you need to take some night classes to bring you up to snuff, then by all means go enroll in an adult education class. If you need to go to the library and pick up a book, by all means dust off that library card and go check out the books you need. If you are Internet savvy, there is so much information that is available to you. Knowledge is just a mouse click away. The point in all of this is to never stop learning. There are so many avenues that we can travel when you have knowledge and access. Knowledge and access are doors of opportunity. The more doors you go through the better chance you have of making all or most of your dreams a reality.

On the path to overcoming shyness or an introverted personality, what you must do is be assertive. I know it may seem difficult but you can do it if you try. You just need to practice. You can improve at anything with practice. At first you will be a bit timid but the more you practice the better you will become at meeting people and shaking off that old attitude.

When you meet someone new, walk right up to them and extend your hand. With a smile on your face and say, "Hi, I am so and so," then follow up with, "it's really nice to meet you." Put yourself in places where you can interact with many people. For instance, if you were to go into a mall setting you have so many opportunities to shake yourself of this intimidated personality. Try different methods of learning how to network with people. You would not believe how fast you will overcome the dread of meeting new people.

Of course noting it will not be an overnight transformation. Changing yourself into an outgoing starfish takes work. When you extend that hand the very first time, you will find that you are on a journey that will help to change your life. You never know who God has put on this earth to be a blessing to you. Networking can open for you vistas that you would have never imagined.

So go ahead, take the plunge. What do you have to lose? The world is yours to conquer. Go out and make something happen. Do not stand by idly, waiting, while everything is happening around you. If anything is going to happen you have to make it happen. Life will pass you by if you just sit and watch. There are three types of people: those who watch things happen, those who make things happen, and those who do not have a clue of what is happening. Do not find yourself in the first or last category. Strive to be with the crowd who are out there making things happen.

I know that even though you can have some disappointments on your quest to be the best. You will one day wake up with things accomplished that you thought could never be achieved. And you will be a happier vibrant person because you had the courage to step out and follow your inward signal. Do not allow your shyness or timid personality to get in your way. Step out.

In life you will meet so many different types of people. The world we live in is very diverse. With so many different cultures you will find that you do not always blend in with the people around you. You must make the effort to learn about other cultures. It is important to know why others behave the way they behave and in doing so you become more tolerant of others.

Since no two people are exactly alike we should not expect that people of various backgrounds to seamlessly blend without a hitch. However we do not have license to think that our way of doing something is the only or best way of getting it done. You must be willing to study others to find what it is that allows them to think and respond in the way that they are responding. Yes, environment has a lot to do with how someone responds, but it is not the only element in the equation.

Different personalities are sometimes brought about because of our genetic structure. But just because your father was an accountant and you work well with numbers does not mean that is the path you are destined to travel. You should try different avenues. And take the same mentality with your children. Allow your children to explore and find the things that work best for them.

All jobs or forms of employment do not fit everyone. But there is something out there for everyone. We must find out where our skills have equipped us to land. Sometimes or should I say most of the time that first job will not be the perfect one. It could however be the stepping stone that leads you down the road to your ultimate achievement.

We must be willing to try new ideas and in the end you will find that your life will be a lot happier and healthier than it would have been had you not taken the chance. So live and try new things and take the information you learn and the experiences you gain and go forth to conquer what you were born to conquer. The key to most people success or the lack thereof, is action.

It is imperative that you get started somewhere on the road to success. On your journey you will encounter roadblocks and snares, but be of good cheer, you will get around it if you keep a positive outlook and stay focused on where it is you are going and what it is you are trying to achieve. Just as everybody wants to see heaven but nobody wants to leave, we all want success and happiness but not everyone wants to put in the time and hard work necessary to achieve it.

I must admit that it is relative but different, what it takes to make me happy and what I consider success. These two things may be vastly different for you as well. But the basic idea is the absence of total conflict in ones life and having more than your needs supplied. As we deal with that concept I submit that a lot of people want happiness and success but are not willing to do what it takes to acquire these positions in life. Most people are not willing to be self-disciplined enough to put off having what they want for a more prosperous future.

When it comes to delayed gratification, which is alien to most people. Most people look at things in the manner of, since it's out there why not start grabbing all I can grab and live life to its fullest? That works but you will miss a lot of future growth. You can have even more. You have to be willing to sacrifice what you have to get more.

Look into things like savings and investments while you are young. Arrange a way for you to have wealth and leisure in your mature years. If you are careful with your finances you will enjoy your senior years. When you are older, after having worked 30-40 years at your career you want to enjoy your life. If you invest early on in life you will not have to work at some dime store at the age of 70 to make ends meet.

Think of perseverance. I will give you an illustration of perseverance. I have another mentor named Claudia Nardone. And Claudia wanted to run her own marketing business but she was afraid. She felt she was inadequate and did not have what it took to run it. But she gave it a try and she stuck it out and was able to navigate her way through the minefield. When the whole world seemed to loom large in her view, backing her in a corner, she came out a winner.

Now Claudia travels around the world allowing other women to feel comfortable in foreign situations that normally make them uncomfortable. She has such a nurturing soul. I have had the privilege of being at a gathering at her home where she made everyone feel comfortable. Claudia went from a shy and timid soul to a world-renowned speaker. When you are in her powerful presence you will not believe how she was able to change her nature. The new Claudia is so self assured and so grounded in her security that she now hosts conventions for groups of women. She allows them to see what is possible for them to achieve if they would only believe and then put some feet to that belief and go after it.

Claudia states in her lectures that she was afraid of her own shadow. She said she was fearful of speaking up and voicing her opinion even when she knew what she had to share was real and something that was needed by the people she would be sharing the information with. Her husband Angelo on numerous occasions has verified the truth of her shyness. And if this timid soul can come out of the shadows and now address a coliseum full of people then you can certainly face whatever obstacle stands in your way. I have come to realize and accept the fact that if you try hard enough and stay in there long enough you can effect change. My hat goes off to you Claudia!

And then there is Fran Hamilton. Fran is another mentor and good example of Integrity.

To know her is to love her. She is so elegant. You will never feel like a stranger after you meet this woman. She will embrace you and allow you to express yourself. She will pull out of you qualities and attributes that you didn't even know you possessed. Fran is the type of person that is comfortable at a $1,000-per plate dinner or in the house with a pair of jeans on putting up wallpaper.

No job is too menial for Fran and no height is above her regal stature. She was made to travel in the circles she has obtained. Fran is a person you would want around when the rest of the world is ready to dump all types of garbage your way. With her in your corner you will be able to transcend boundaries that before seemed unreachable. She will inspire you to go forth and just try one more time.

Don't get me wrong, Fran will cut you with a word of truth. She will tell you like it is smile and walk away. You will not even know you are bleeding until you become lightheaded and faint from the loss of blood. She is capable of discipline also, she is no soft touch. If the situation calls for a strong hand she is more than capable of showing up. Fran was brought up in the church and was given a basic foundation of how to deal with your brothers and sisters. She knows how to be fair and equitable in the different types of situations that will develop while trying to negotiate your way through this life. She is quick to let you know from her past and vast experience that if she can make it, so can you.

In life you will experience failure at one thing or another and how you deal with the setback will determine the extent you will grow in your endeavor to succeed. Everyone faces times when things do not go according to plan. The question then becomes, do we sit there and whine or complain that this should not be happening to me, wallow in our self-defeating behavior. Or do we acknowledge it and move on? Do not get me wrong it is all right to acknowledge failure or a setback. But use it to keep growing and learning. We can learn from our mistakes when we review how or where it went wrong. But to replay it over and over, beating yourself up because you have miscalculated the outcome is not the right direction to head in. At a time like that you must pick yourself up, dust yourself off and start all over again.

We can look at our situation, make a diagnosis, grow from it and move on. Then move forward headed in the right direction. We can not allow our setbacks to determine our direction or when we will get there. A setback is just a temporary roadblock designed to slow you down so you can begin to see the situation in its true light and deal with it more effectively. Look at the big picture or at least what you have in front of you and evaluate what type of an affect the setback will have on the efforts you have put forth and what affect it will have on the final outcome. But after having observed then move on.

We must be sure to distance ourselves from the disease of making excuses for our lack of accomplishment. All too often we get caught up in blaming everyone or everything for our lack of performance. Don't go pointing the finger at everyone else. Direct the blame at the person who is really at fault. When it comes to victory we want all the acclaim, we don't want to share the spotlight with anyone. So when it comes to failure be as equally selfish. Take it all for yourself.

I am here this day at this time to remind you that you must inform yourself that the buck stops here. Whatever heights you climb or achieve it will be up to you. Whatever depths you descend to are because of your lack of effort. We must realize that we are where we are in life because of the choices we have made up to this point. Life is choice driven and we must be willing to accept the outcome of the choices that we have made. Once we have accepted that position then we can move on with our lives and start to make provisions for change.

You do not go to the doctor unless you have symptoms of some sort. And everyone knows how expensive medical treatment can be. But once you have symptoms you go seek professional help to try and rid yourself of anything that does not agree with the way you are supposed to feel. Much like the health of our body we must acknowledge that we are responsible for our mental wellbeing as well. When we realize this we are able to put the reigns on our mind and control our own destiny. If you do not accept the fact that you are in control you can never affect change.

Chapter Twelve

Go to God for Endurance

We have the power within to be all that we can be and we must draw on that power at every turn. Too often we look for others to make us happy or successful and in reality that is not going to happen. If we are going to be happy or successful it will be as a result of something that we have decided to accomplish. Take the bull by the horns and wrestle him down to receive the victory ring. No one can do it for us. We must do whatever we know to do, and if we do not know what to do, just do something until you get a true vision as to what your purpose and destiny truly is.

"If any of you lack wisdom, let him ask of God that giveth to all men liberally..."[37] We have help we just need to ask for it. When we humble ourselves then our gracious, loving, heavenly Father can come in and exalt us. When you get to the place where you know you are not capable of doing it by yourself go to God. Ask, not wavering, and believe that He will do it for you. Before you know it you will be on your way to achieving things in life that up to this point you would have never dreamed were possible.

When we fall behind schedule some people use that as an excuse to quit and give up on their dreams and aspirations. But that is not the time to give up but a time to give out. We are to give out of our abundance and gather our strength of purpose and move on towards the intended goal. A setback is a set up for your next victory campaign. The enemy will throw little hurdles or roadblocks in the way to get you to give up and throw in the towel. But if you keep your feet to the metal at these times you will witness a breakthrough that can propel you to the highest level of human experience. Right before daylight the sky appears to be its darkest. When things appear to be all out of control or discombobulated, do not give up. Do not give in either, but look out over the horizon and you will begin to see the breaking of a new day. And with each new day will bring new opportunities to work on your destiny and purpose for being here on this planet.

When you are on the path to freedom or success, you will face obstacles and at times you might tend to want to give up, turnaround or just throw in the towel. At times you become bewildered, thinking you have no other alternatives. But if you just hold on you will find that obstacles are designed to build you up and bring out the best in your character. If everything were laid out on a silver platter you would not know what you were truly capable of overcoming. But now that challenges arise in your life you must come up with alternative answers that will define who you really are.

Another saying goes, "When the going gets tough, the tough gets going." [38] That phrase is another way of saying "don't give up." Hold up, don't rust out but allow yourself to get worn out. When all is said and done you did all that you had the opportunity to achieve. You lived your life to the fullest and have no regrets. That can only be said of those who see the obstacles as a challenge but go around, over, under or through. You must continue to strive until you succeed because nothing will come to a quitter except a bunch of empty dreams and you will not be satisfied with emptiness all around you. So be determined to take it all the way. Do not allow anything or anyone to stop you from reaching the purpose that has been given to you.

Maintain your commitment and continue to strive toward fulfilling your purpose. If you stay committed you will not be denied. One day you will realize your ultimate goals and aspirations. Many people quit along the way but only because they have not committed themselves to see their plan through to fruition. But you are in this thing to win. You will be victorious in your pursuit of purpose. You will achieve what God has ordained for you from the foundation of the earth. Believe that you were created to achieve greatness and only you can allow the enemy to defeat you. You have been equipped to overcome every obstacle that the wicked one produces. So be a glory producer and make it happen.

When you continue to push forward you will find that you will have a renewed strength. There is something that happens to each of us when we persevere. It is like the runner who gets their second wind, enabling them to run harder and faster to go on to win the race. With only a minute or so left in the race their legs felt like they were ready to burst. Their legs were giving the signal that they could not run another step. But because they were able to push through they were given a whole new set of reserve energy. And that is what allowed them to win in the end.

I say to you, that if you do not give up there will be exciting vistas out there that you will conquer and be able to look back and realize that because you persisted, you were able to come out victorious. But had you given up and thrown in the towel you would have forever been beating up on yourself saying what you could have achieved if you would have continued on the path that you were on. Instead of having to look back with regret, look forward to the whole array of possibilities that loom so large ahead of you. Go for it and you will not be disappointed. I dare say that you will end up being pleasantly surprised if anything.

We must get a view of what it is we would like to accomplish and stay focused on that. When we go to the word of God, the word states that, "Where there is no vision the people perish..." [39] This is precisely why we strive to maintain the vision that has been presented and we nurture that vision into manifestation. You must venture to work diligently towards the furtherance of your full potential to realize what God has in-store for you. In trying to realize your vision you must continue to move in the direction of the information that is given. Do not stop just because you do not have all the answers at the start of your journey. You do not need the grace to finish the project until you start on your road to success. The vision will keep you moving and help to move those hindrances out of your way. When you become a little weary and worn down along the way go to God and you will receive sustaining grace to keep you moving along.

You will not need the grace to finish the course until you have already run the race and have come to a point where you feel you have nothing left. That is when you will receive the grace to finish. Up to this point there was no need for it. When you are in the last stretch of the race and all seems lost, the help will then be there to complete it. When you learn to trust our Creator, that is when He will step in and do for you what you can not do for yourself. Our God is faithful and He will be there at the times that you need Him the most. This thought reminds me of the poem footprints. When you think that you are all alone, that is when He is there to lift your heavy burdens and to help you along the way. Our God is a God you can always call on and I want to be a witness that you can always depend on him because He is faithful and always near.

The road to success is fraught with distractions and you must not allow yourself to become desensitized by the bumps in the road. It has been said that "success is a journey not a destination" [40] and while we are on the journey we must not allow the glare of the lights or the glitter of the stage to sidetrack us and forfeit what it is that we were destined in this life to achieve. It is like the peanut butter on the little mousetrap. The little fellow is so overwhelmed by the fragrance of the delightful morsel he is about to take advantage of, that he does not see the big trap that is about to snap its neck. That is why we must stay focused and not become sidetracked by the things that have no true future value.

Some things come into your space to take you off course. We all have a divine purpose and that is why it is vitally important to keep that in mind as you go towards your future. The enemy comes to steal, kill and destroy and he does not care how he does it. He might put anything in your path with the intent to throw you off course and send you into orbit. It may first be some small thing that gets your attention. But if you are not careful, before long it is vying for more and more attention. Before you know it you have become consumed, spending all of your valuable time pursuing things other than what God has ordained for you to achieve. It is the little foxes that destroy the vine.

When obstacles come to steal your attention, they do not always show up as an obstacle and that is why they are able to get in your life. If you are not paying attention, boom! You are caught up. So beware of those things that try to get your attention and have you putting off for tomorrow what you should be attending to today. You will be successful because you did not allow the negative aspects of your past keep you from reaching your potential for success. Everyone has something in their past that they are not proud of. But do not allow it to hold you back from reaching your full potential.

You are the person you are because of all the choices you have made in your life up to this point. Only you can allow your past to dictate to you what your future will become. Some people will look at the things that have happened in the past and continue to beat themselves up for it. Others even will try to dictate to them what they cannot accomplish because of past failures. Just remember, you can utilize the things in your past to propel you toward your ultimate goals. Allow past errors to be learning experiences along the way to a brighter future.

The problem is not getting off course. It is reported that most pilots are off course for most of their flights, and still end up reaching the destination. No, the problem comes when we do not take the time to address the issue and take corrective actions. Making sure that once you discover that you are not where you are suppose to be, that you will start to tweak the process. Turn off and head in the direction that would be most conducive to reaching or achieving the desired results. We who are on the road to achievement must constantly monitor our progress to make sure that we are making the most expedient use of our time and talents. These types of actions will help us to be more efficient and more effective.

One thing that is certain about life is that it has a way of becoming overwhelming. If you do not take it little at a time, before you know it all types of situations will creep in and catch you unaware. But when life becomes too overpowering and you find that you are at the end of your rope, take the rope, tie it around your waist and hold on. Situations that develop in your life will come and go. You will get through them. Then later when you look back you will find that you learned a great lesson from your trials and tribulations. Do not run from them seek the lesson to be learned.

We go through cycles in life. Sometimes life is going real good. Everything seems to be clicking on all thirty-two valves and life as you know it is one big party. Then there are the other days where it seems that nothing wants to come together for you and you want to take your vehicle and head for the nearest cliff. In both of these situations what you must learn to do is practice poise. Life will change again. It is never going to continue to be on peaks or stay down in the valley. You have to just remember that in life there will be changes. Know that some days will be good and others will not be so good. But you can win this race if you will just stay the course. Do not allow yourself to get sidetracked with the situation. Keep doing the small mundane things and it will work itself out in its season.

In our endeavors to pursue excellence the enemy will come at us like a flood. But don't be disheartened because the very God we are serving says that "...the Spirit of the Lord shall lift up a standard against him." [41] When we look around at every turn and see nothing but challenges coming at us, chances are the enemy is coming against you and what you stand for. He is trying to make you take your eyes off the promises of God. If he can get you to the bend or doubt God then he has succeeded at his goal. But we do not have to allow him the victory in our life. We must remain steadfast and unmovable, always abounding in the work of the Lord.

Often times you must stand tall in the face of adversity and continue down the path of what you feel is right, even if the whole world has a different opinion than what you feel is right for you. Consider Bill Gates for instance, he dropped out of school to pursue his dreams. Can you imagine how many people were probably telling him how foolish his idea was to drop out school his junior year, with one more year of college remaining. For someone else, and I do mean a lot of someone else's, that would have been brilliant advice, but not for Bill Gates. You see he followed his heart, and now has one of the largest, if not the largest computer firm in the world known as Microsoft. So follow your heart. But if it takes you off course and you see a dead end, it is all right to stop and admit you was on the wrong course and change directions to get back in stride.

Even when we find ourselves in a position of major setbacks we must still try to work on our situation from a biblical perspective. We have to do it God's way. And just because money is a little tight we cannot neglect to do what God has already ordained. We have been directed to bring our tithes and offering into the storehouse and allow the Lord to open the windows of heaven and pour us out a blessing that we do not have room enough to receive it. [42] We must give. The word says "Give and it shall be given unto you..." [43] but we must give with the right attitude. We must have a cheerful heart, and when you cheerfully give you are planting seed. God is able to take those seeds and cause increase taking you to the next level in your giving. In life you will also have financial mishaps and they will tend to throw you off of your schedule of giving. They may send you in a tailspin. But we must not allow those things that cause interference to be the dominating process.

In any situation, when you realize that you are off task you should refocus and continue on the set journey. Continue to monitor your goals and objectives on a daily basis. Keep your objective in front of you. This process is so vital to your future growth because if you do not review your goals daily you could be off course and not realize it until you are far off course of where it is you are headed. But once you realize where you are, do not sit in gloom and doom. Get up, dust yourself off and get on with your goals and aspirations.

Chapter Thirteen

Step Out and Find Your True Destiny

When things seem to come at us from all directions and it seems that there is just no way out we must find the way to rejoice in the midst of the turmoil. The truth being told, it is only a test, a test to see what you are made of. How will your endurance capacity hold up? The God we serve says that he will never put any more on us then we are capable of handling. When you get into situations that you see the light at the end of the tunnel and what appears to be a freight train, just remember it is not. But what it is may be of help, direction to show you the way to proceed. What is most interesting is that once you reach the light, the answer to most of your issues will present themselves to you. So keep on being steadfast, continue to move with a positive state of mind.

Of course you could be thinking how I could be positive with all the turmoil that is going on around me. The answer will still be the same, this is only a test. In the end you will reap if you faint not. So brighten up, your day is coming. For a reference point, read Job chapters 1 and 2, and you will see an example of a person who went through every imaginable, horrible situation that you could possibly deal with. But when you get into the story you will find that Job maintained his integrity. He realized that the God he served is an awesome God. And one of the things Job said was, "Though He slay me, yet will I trust in him..." [44]

Now you talk about integrity, Job is one who exemplified integrity. The question begs to ask. Did he survive the torment and was he able to overcome? Well if you go to the end of the book, you will see that our God is faithful. He will perform that which he has promised. In the midst of his trials and tribulations Job made the assessment, in Job 36:11 that, "If they (we) obey and serve Him, they (we) shall spend their (our) days in prosperity and their (our) years in pleasures." So yes we will be rewarded for maintaining our trust in the one true God. We must be loyal to the process. We must strive to be on target. When we find ourselves in a situation that seems to cause stress and turmoil, our first thought might be to turn and leave it alone. But when we find ourselves not giving in to the pressures of life we find that opportunity will present itself to those who prevail.

Bishop Lorenzo Turner is one such individual. He was born in Memphis, Tennessee on the impoverished side of town, but grew up in Chicago, Illinois on the rough side of town. His parents moved there to seek better opportunities for supporting a family. Upon settling in, the family found living in Chicago was not a picnic. Lorenzo recalls days when the rat-infested apartment (I do emphasize rats, not mice.) were determined to take over the house. The rats were so big, that the cats were afraid.

At age twelve, Lorenzo was hit by a car which left him bedridden for almost a year in a full-body cast. Shortly after recovering from that trauma, Lorenzo was struck down by another car, both times disobeying his mother about running out in the street.

Lorenzo's mother thought that the Chicago gangs would have too much of an influence on her eight children, six young impressionable sons and two daughters; that she felt she had to get her boys out of the city before they became statistics. The family moved from Chicago to Rock Island, Illinois where Lorenzo discovered a young lady named Toni. She eventually became his wife and the mother of their four children. While in a Rock Island high school, Lorenzo discovered he had a natural talent for the game of football. Because of his attention to details, he was able to make something good happen every time he was on the field. This talent caught the eyes of the college recruiters from Oklahoma State University who began a campaign to lure him to their campus.

Lorenzo Turner helped Oklahoma State win the 1976 conference championship and later the Tangerine Bowl. That championship propelled him to the locker room of the Dallas Cowboys, the British Columbian Lions and the Detroit Lions. He now sees that the success he achieved, the devil meant for bad by the pitfalls he put in his path. But God was able to be glorified through it. While he was a superstar, all types of money flowed in his direction. With money came many opportunities, some to destroy everything he had established up to this point. But because he was not grounded in the Lord at this time, the bags of money went through his hands like coffee through a filter.   Lorenzo found himself on his way to Detroit to try out for the Detroit Lions, instead it turned out he would pastor a nationwide ministry which was based in the northern suburbs of Detroit. God sent him to Detroit to prepare him for work that he would do in the ministry.

Providence has a way of showing up when we least expect it. As talented as Lorenzo was he just didn't make the grade with the Detroit Lions, even after giving them his best effort. After being shut out and having been relieved of all his worldly assets through a lot of foolish decisions, Lorenzo was faced with the prospect of obtaining gainful employment to support his wife and children. He obtained gainful employment, though the job was not the cure all it was something he could sink his teeth into. After a few years, lateral moves became available giving Lorenzo more experience and knowledge.

As fate would have its way, Toni, Lorenzo's wife was converted to the holiness movement. Because of her consistent prayers and her chaste behavior after becoming saved, was the catalyst that caused Lorenzo to change and get to know more of that movement she was a part of.

Toni is consistently praying for others who are facing challenges, and God is still answering her prayers. Toni was also involved in the union of Marsha and I becoming one. To this day, Toni says that she has never suggested any one get married besides my wife and me.

Because of his talents for football it was hard for him to let go of the football dreams and aspirations. While going through a lot of unnecessary struggles Lorenzo were forced to realize that when God has a call on your life, the best thing you can do is surrender. He did that and allowing God to have total control of his life, Lorenzo was rewarded with the honor of being an elder, a pastor and finally a bishop with churches that he oversees in Michigan, Chicago, Iowa and soon in Rock Island, Illinois.

To this day Lorenzo Turner is quick to say that God has a way of elevating those who keep their minds focused on Him. When we focus on what is right and are determined to go where it is He has destined for us, there is nothing that could keep us from having what God wants for us. From the rat-infested ghettos in Chicago to the prosperous suburbs of Detroit, then from store front churches to a million dollar building with an expansive outreach, I would say that Bishop Lorenzo Turner is now walking in God's will. But it is because of his devotion to finding his purpose. Nothing comes to a quitter but empty cupboards. But to the man who will go the extra mile, he will find his table is overflowing.

Opportunities sometimes come in a package that seems like it will be an unfair exchange. But if we delve a little deeper we will find the gems that we have been searching for. A diamond may start off as a lump of coal. But because of time and the persistence of miners we find ourselves enjoying the fruits of their labor. We take pleasure in sporting our diamond rings, necklaces and brooches. At the outset, who would have paid 10, 20, 50 thousand dollars for a lump of coal?

You must explore opportunities when they come up and you might discover that you have already been given your backyard filled with fruit bearing trees. Do not give up just because the road gets a little rough sometimes. Just tuck it in, gird up the loins of your mind and trudge ahead. You will find that you will gain strength of purpose along the way if you would just keep your eyes on the prize. It is there for you, and all who would but dare go out and discover their true seed of greatness.

Because of your persistence you will be able to accomplish things that others find they cannot obtain. A little effort put in the right direction will take you a long way. You can achieve a lot more because you refuse to sit down and give up on the process. Most people quit in the middle of the struggle to find that others pass them by on the road to the top. If you see yourself going into a rut start to refocus on your dreams and the things in life that mean the most to you. This will help you to generate energy that should pump you up to continue in the direction in which you were headed before you went into a stall.

Many people get knocked down and stay down, they count themselves out. You see a lot of that on the streets in the summer time or at the refuge centers in the wintertime. Now by no stretch of the imagination am I saying that everyone who is down and out has refused to get back up. But I am saying too often when we see people that we call homeless or bag people. Most of these people were dealt a setback at some point and did not know how to handle it. They allowed it to hinder their recovery. Accept the fact that we will not win every battle. But we can be sure that if we keep getting up, time after time we will win the war. Stay in the battle, because you are going to come out victorious if you keep at it.

Our challenges only come to test our faith. We know that when they come we can run to the rock of our foundation. We can go to the word. In the word of God is the answer to any and every situation that may develop in your life. There is always a way of escape. It might be obscure but if we search it out we will find what we are looking for. We will succeed because we were persistently pursuing a faith walk and believing that we would ultimately reach the goal if we continue to persevere. One word of encouragement can go a long way to someone who is experiencing a setback. Some time all they need to hear is that positive message, letting them know they can make it. The fact that you tell them that you believe in them will help to lift their spirits, which in turn could put them back on the road to success.

It is really easy to get shipwrecked when you lose your momentum. All types of negative thoughts try to bombard your mind, giving you reasons of why you will fail. That is why it is so important for others to reach out with words of kindness, words of hope. Some people need to hear that if they just keep trying, keep moving forth, in the end they will succeed at their endeavor. Every opportunity you should tell someone to "don't give up hope; keep your dream alive." When we give others words of encouragement it will help to keep them on the right path. Sometimes we all can get a little down and depressed because the world seems to be caving in on us. But that word of hope can help ease the weight off your shoulders and lighten the burdens.

We can help lighten the load of our brothers and sisters by being a burden carrier which would help to alleviate some of the stress. When you share the burden it definitely makes for a lighter load on the person who was carrying the weight of it all. When nothing seems to be going right all you need to do is call on the name of the Lord and He will be there right away. And when you call upon that name you will find that He is more than able, He is willing to come to your aid, when you need Him the most. God is your Jehovah Jireh and he will provide for you comfort in the midnight hour, peace when all around you seems to be in disarray, joy when all hope is lost.

My God is capable of being whatever you need Him to be and the thing about our Lord, is that it doesn't take all day to reach Him. He is not some absentee dead Lord as some would have you believe. No, He is a right now God who will be there for you. He loves for you to call on His name. The next time you need a friend call on my friend, the Lord and Savior Jesus Christ. He "… is a friend that sticketh closer than a brother." [45] He'll be there for you.

Fear of the unknown will have a devastating effect on how you live your life if you do not get a grip on it. Instead of running from every challenge and new situation because you fear what the outcome will be, I suggest you embrace the unknown and take the chance. "There is nothing to fear but fear itself? [46] Go for it, whatever it may be. If it is continuing your education, go to the school and find out what is needed to enroll. Take the first step towards achieving your goal and you will find that it was not some big hairy monster waiting in the dark to pounce all over you.

Let's say you have always wanted to take a stab at golfing but were fearful, unsure of yourself. Well make the call and find out where you can take lessons from an in-house pro. Find you a driving range to practice and let it go. The purpose in finding the golf pro to teach you is so that you don't learn bad habits from the beginning. Because once you learn them you will get better and better at performing them and they will become intrinsically harder to break. So learn right from the beginning and you will be so much farther ahead. Most people get stuck in the shadows, afraid to step out and find their true destiny, or greatness. Fear is such a debilitating force that you must fight hard to not allow it to envelope you completely.

The fear factor starts off as such a small thought. As we begin to think on it, it becomes embedded in our subconscious mind. Then we compound the thoughts adding more and more ammunition for the assault team to work against you. What you must do is remind yourself that it is only a thought and it has nothing to do with who you are and how you live your daily life. Take control and cast it out, move on to a more positive satisfying train of thought. Remember the acronym for fear is **F**alse, **E**vidence **A**ppearing **R**eal. That acronym fits because fear itself is not something that is real. It is all in your imagination. To be up front and brutally truthful, it is just a waste of your precious time. No matter how much you fear it is not going to change the outcome anyhow. So go ahead and make it happen in spite of the fear.

When fear is viewed from that perspective, whatever "it" is becomes a little more tolerable, a little bit easier to handle. The "it" represents the fear or the thing that you are apprehensive about, and it is not real. What you need to do is examine what "it" is that is making you afraid and tackle the issue head on. You must approach it from the standpoint of, "I can do this thing". No matter what happens I will face my fear.

You are probably saying this may be easier said than done. But what happens when I am face-to-face with a foul mouth adversary in a meeting, and I'm the person with the soft-spoken timid personality? You will have to stand your ground. Admit to yourself that you are a little timid in this situation but you will have to handle yourself somehow and you will. And in doing this, you will be on the road to dealing with the butterflies that you find in the pit of your stomach when you face challenging situations. You will just teach your butterflies to not be scattered in all directions, but to lineup in formation.

We all get butterflies in different situations no matter who we are. The butterflies are there because we want to do a good job and that shows that you are concerned about how well you do. So you take that nervous energy and use it to help make you better. You would not be apprehensive if you didn't care. So now that you know why something is happening take the ball in hand and grab control. Deal with the situation. I know it is new and I know it is different. But I also know that if you would just go forward you will be able to handle the situation at hand. And after having faced the challenge you will be more equipped the next time you are facing a harrowing episode in your life.

Perhaps the reason for the fear is that we feel that we are not worthy or we do not have the skills or know how to make something happen. If you stop and think about it, the person who has the job you want now did not have the skills either at one time, or the know how. But he or she did not allow that to hinder his or her progress and neither should you. A key to growth and success is that you look for opportunities and just go for it. You can pick up the essentials on your way to the top. You must be willing to look defeat in the face and continue on without allowing it to get you down and throw you out of the race. For only then will you be in a position to achieve greatness. And your greatness will not be measured by how many times you get knocked down, but in how many times you get back up.

When the adversities of life get to be burdensome and there seems to be no way out, just look to God and go to the Father of hope. Our God is sufficient to handle all of our aches and pains. The Word of God says that He would never leave us or forsake us. And you can rest in that promise. Because God's word is a sure word and His Angels hasten to perform it. He said that He esteems His word above His name. The word says, "That at the name of Jesus every knee shall bow... and that every tongue should confess that Jesus Christ is Lord, to the glory of God the Father." [47] You can rest assured that God will see you through to completion.

We must have a commitment to our dreams and aspirations, not with speech only but with actions. Until we put forth some kind of action we are only dealing with rhetoric and that is worth as much as a pound of hot air. It will get you as far as the couch in front of the TV when it comes to reaching your goals. We must be people of vision. Once we realize the vision of where it is we would like to go, we can put forth the momentum towards the goal.

Commitment is not taking no for an answer. If there is some obstacle in the way, commitment says that I will find a way around it, over it, or through it. And in the end I will have reached my destiny. You were destined for greatness. So go for it and while on your journey you might have setbacks but you can know that because of your commitment to realize your goal there will be nothing or no one that will stop you from getting there. And as you navigate through life you should take time to reflect on past experiences. And while reflecting you will find that your good times out weighed your bad times and you should consider yourself blessed.

In life no matter who you are or what background you came from, it is for certain you will have challenges in your life. Knowing this, all you can hope to do is overcome the little hiccups along the way and proceed forth. Just because we do not feel like doing something does not give us the right to shun our responsibilities. We are on a team and must pick up the baton and run with it, the team needs us. Garner enough strength to put something in motion. Once we start going in a forward direction we will find that it creates momentum of its own.

When we participate in life, life has a tendency to reward us for our efforts and punish or deny us for the lack thereof. That is why we must get into the race and allow life to run its course. Find some way to enjoy life. If you do not like yourself, then you are probably a heavy load on others. If you talk failure, telling people about how bad life is, and how you have been dealt an unfair hand you will live what you speak. Life is not fair. It will deal to you what you put into it and nothing more. So shake off the dust and get on with the job of living. Life is too short to spend all of it whining and complaining.

Remember when everybody wanted to "be like Mike" — Michael Jordan that is. Many companies paid him big bucks to endorse their products because he is one of the most recognizable athletes in the world. But that was not always the case. When Mike was a 5-foot-9 sophomore in high school he was cut from the varsity basketball team. By his junior year his height had jumped to 6-foot-3 and he was back on the team. By his senior year he was an all-state guard. From there he went on to North Carolina, became an All-American earning player of the year accolades his sophomore and junior years. [48] He would eventually lead the Tar Heels to an NCAA championship and the Chicago Bulls to an unprecedented six World Championship titles. Now Mike could have given up, thrown in the towel when he was cut from the team in high school. If he had, the world would have missed out on one of the best trained, most disciplined athletes in history. Instead, because of his determination, he was able to accomplish amazing feats that most people could only dream about.

In my efforts to give accolades to those who have gone before us to initiate change, whether political, social, or economical. My list would be incomplete if I was not to include the valiant contributions of the late great Dr. Martin Luther King, Jr. He used his life as an instrument to bring about change in our society during a turbulent time in our nation's history. Dr. King studied the life of Gandhi and figured he could make a bigger impact on people's lives utilizing a nonviolent agenda. Raised in the south in a middle-class family, he did not see his color as a reason to not be treated as an equal. He was a man of vision. In his "I Have a Dream" speech, a speech that would rock America and go down in the annals of history as being one of the most profound yet provocative speeches of all time. He touched people of all nationalities: black, white, Hispanic, Asian, and Jews. We are all apart of the human race and his agenda was for us as a people to be able to sit down together and live in unity. As we continue into the 21st Century, some of his vision has come to pass. But we are a people who still have a long, long road to travel.

Think about the Nazi concentration camps? What would inspire someone to commit mass genocide? On the other hand what would give someone the strength to pack up their things after seeing their parents carted off to death camps to be annihilated? It took fortitude. As a young man, he and his aunt put money together to give to the leader of the group. They could not help but feel a tinge of fear as they thought of how this could end up. On one hand they could end up in the death camps like the other countless millions who had gone before them, or they could believe and hope for the impossible.

As the fear gripped their hearts, the group huddled in silent anticipation that they would be discovered. But when they considered the choices, they knew that they must continue on marching through the night. Their hope became stronger and stronger with each step taken. And as they reached the border to another country, the money was exchanged and they were allowed to walk on through and continue on into the interior of the countryside, ultimately were taken in as refugees. Imagine what a joyous time they have had since walking in freedom. The pain of lost loved ones can never be erased. How can you forget such brutality? Somehow you find a way to put it behind you and hope that history like that never repeats itself.

This goes back to the premise of, when we believe in something strong enough we will find a way to make it happen. So garner your strength and muster up your courage and dust off all your dreams and aspirations. You can achieve your dreams if you would just believe. Then put your actions with it and go out and do something toward it. Little incremental steps at first, but I guarantee if you take enough steps you will ultimately reach whatever it was you set out to do.

It's like the old adage, "How do you eat an elephant? You eat it one bite at a time." If you look at the big picture you might become overwhelmed and do nothing. You may get frozen in fear but if you break it down into smaller bite-size components, then you can logically see it coming to fruition thereby alleviating your fears. As you read through the pages of this book you will begin to see how some ordinary people did some extraordinary things because they refused to lend their minds to negative thinking. The element that all these people have in common is the fact that somewhere down on the inside, they mustered the strength to say yes when everything about them said no, this is not supposed to happen. But they persisted in moving forward and you will notice that time after time they were able to transform their lives. And not only that, they were also able to impact those people who came in contact with them.

The mind is a terrible thing to waste. But if you harvest your thought process, it will take you to heights you can only imagine. Just know, in the end, whether you win or lose, whether you obtain that lofty goal, or be denied, will depend on the effort you put forth. More importantly, it will depend on how you maintain control over your thought process. How will you be able to keep the negative forces at bay, those self-defeating thoughts that will keep you groveling at the bottom of the pile? You must continue to affirm what it is you are striving to obtain. "Mr. Negative" will constantly bombard you with thoughts of why you can not achieve your goals. You must speak positive affirmations consistently to counter the negatives. You must set up a strategic battlefield in order to fight back.

When the negatives come in they will bombard you with all types of reasons why what you're doing can not be done. That is why it is imperative that you have an offense to counter the negative effect. The way you prepare for the onslaught is association with positive others and read books. The people who are going to lead us into the next battle front are the readers. When you find a reader you will be witnessing a leader. All leaders are people who are well versed. Association with those people who are like-minded will help to keep you on track with where it is you are headed.

Find you a nucleus of mentors who are going where you want to go or who have already arrived at where you would like to be. If you are going to successfully navigate a minefield, then follow in the path of those who have successfully reached their destination. You do not have to always recreate the wheel. All you need to do is follow in the path of those who have already obtained the end result. When you set in your heart something that you would like to achieve there are two things that play a vital role in you receiving it. One is persistence and the second is determination. Both of these are a part of your frame of mind. But when you have made up your mind that you will not be denied, no matter what, you will not be. When the mountains loom in the horizon, you will act like water and go around, over, or under. And if all else fails you must be ready to go through that mountain.

That is where persistence comes into play. When you are persistent, things start to happen. That is because you did not give up.

Doors will begin to open, and things will seem to become a little more tolerable. You will probably have a little more energy too but that is no accident. Your mind was made to function like that. The more we put into a situation the more we will get out of it. Because we have been persistent in reaching our goal, we become better equipped along the way.

I have heard that practice makes perfect, but I have also witnessed that practice makes permanent. If you are practicing your golf swing but from the beginning you have the wrong posture and the wrong grip, after 10 years you will have done a lot of hard work and chances are you are never going to swing your club in the pro circuit. So what you must do is practice. Know from the start of any endeavor that it is good to start off on the right foot. And if you do that and continue to place one foot in front of the other you will meet up with your destiny. Life is full of surprises. Just hope that in the end the surprise will be a rewarding, exhilarating experience that others will be able to learn and prosper from.

Chapter Fourteen

Final Thoughts

When life is all said and done and we are granted the opportunity to reflect back over the years and review all the decisions we have made. We will find that a lot of things we were so concerned with were blown way out of proportion. If in this life we could adopt the mindset of "don't worry over the little things," we would be better off. Because in relation to the whole scheme of things, the little things we are up against are really nothing at all. They loom large on the horizon and they appear to be some big hairy monster but upon closer inspection we find that we were able to handle the issue. With careful thought and planning we can take on every situation that develops in our life, without panicking and acting irrationally.

We must strive to be people of integrity. As we go through our daily tasks the one thing that we must have as our guiding light is integrity. Integrity is what you do when you think no one is looking or is going to know about it. You must walk according to the truth. Do not let the world tell you to skim a little off the top and from people all-around you. Listen to the small voice that is telling you to rise up, be different and follow your conscious. You will expand or be consumed by the choices you make. So make the right choice. Live and listen to the still small voice, which is the voice of conscious.

If you do not listen when it is trying to lead you in the right direction, you put yourself in a position to end up with a seared conscious. Then you will not be able to hear anything about right or wrong good or bad. Don't ignore your conscious and it will always lead you down the right road, which is straight and narrow.

What we say should match up with what we do. When people hear from our mouth that we believe in such and such, our actions should line up with our verbiage. When we do what we say people will have more confidence in the things you say to them. But more important than that, is the fact that you will have more confidence in yourself. When you say something and consistently follow up with contradictory actions, your self-esteem index will plummet. Your conscience will not rest if you go about, living a lie. The truth about who you really are will eat away at your self-worth. Do the right thing every time you have the opportunity — just remember if you do for someone else the way you expect them to do for you, you will do it better.

We must look to Jesus who is the author and finisher of our faith whenever situations develop that we have no control over. When everything seems to be going anyway but the right way He will give you peace in the midst of the storms of life that come to test your faith. Satan tempts you to turn you away from trusting in the Almighty God. When everything and everyone seems to go the opposite of what you expect, just know you serve a mighty God who will gird you up and protect you, "He that dwelleth in the secret place of the Most High, shall abide under the shadow of the Almighty." [49] God has your back.

You don't have to run away in defeat, no, you can stand flat-footed and face the onslaught of the enemy. You can stand still and see the salvation of the Lord just as Moses told the children of God when they were facing the Red Sea and the Egyptians were in hot pursuit. In their mindset they saw doom and destruction and that is what happens to us when we get bombarded by situation after situation and there appears to be no answer. I say to you, be of good courage, my God can rescue you if you would just put your confidence in him; take your eyes off the problem and focus them on the solution which is available to those who trust Him for an answer and he can deliver you out of any situation whether big or small.

The enemy will have you thinking that there is no hope or chance to come up with a solution to your dilemma. Please remember that he is a liar and the father of lies. You can not believe what he is trying to say to you. The question is what information are you going to believe? For me and my family we have decided to believe the Word of the Lord.

The enemy comes to steal the seed of faith that you have in our savior. So in the midst of what you are doing he will throw all types of discord and disharmony your way. But when you get to the end of your rope, tie it around your waist and just hold on because help is just a request away. Our God is a God who responds to faith. The book of Hebrew states, "But without faith it is impossible to please Him, for he that cometh to God must believe that He is and that He is a rewarder of them who diligently seek Him." [50] And right now just check up on your faith walk. Remember you are the one who determines if you will respond in faith or fear, God has equipped you to know Him.

The void that we have in our innermost being, which never seems to be filled, can only, be filled with the one and only true God, Jesus the Christ. For, "Our God is a Spirit and they that worship Him must worship Him in Spirit and in truth." [51] So get in the spirit, and get to know the truth; that my God is able to deliver you from any and all situations that the enemy has come to ensnare you with. As we are going through life, we will all be faced with situations that may be a little more than what we are prepared to bite off at the time. But if we would just look at the circumstances from God's eyes we would have a different perspective.

Our God knows the beginning from the ending. We will not feel so overwhelmed knowing that our God has it all in control. There is nothing that happens that He is not aware of. And it can't happen unless He allows it to happen. Once you have settled in your heart that God has your best interest at heart, you can relax and begin to enjoy the life that you are destined to live. We must learn to live in peace and harmony with those around us instead of always striving to be on top of one another. A group working in unity, even if they are smaller will produce more than a much larger group who is at odds, because they are working in harmony.

You must strive to be a team player, there is no "I" in team. Check your ego at the door and give it up to the team effort and you will see a change in you and your environment.

We must learn to appreciate the small things that we have already obtained because for the most part people tend to think that they can not rejoice and give a victory shout unless they have accomplished some gigantic feat. We should not only rejoice in the bigger things but we should shout the victory and give praise for all of our successes. In Deuteronomy 8:18 the word says that, "But thou shalt remember the Lord thy God: for it is he that giveth thee power to get wealth, that he may establish his covenant which he **sware** unto thy fathers as it is this day."

When we give thanks we are showing appreciation for what has been done for us. And when the praises go up, the blessings shall surely flow down. In our not too distance past, perhaps we did things we didn't feel were favorable. Yet we keep pulling those past negative episodes into our present, allowing them to hinder our progress. We end up developing a guilt complex and try to convince ourselves subconsciously that we are not worthy of success because of our past behavior. You must put that way of thinking in the trash because its only purpose is to hinder you from moving on in life and accomplishing your God-given purpose. John 10:10 says that, "The thief cometh not, but for to steal, kill and to destroy: I come that they might have life and that they might have it more abundantly," so choose Jesus and choose life.

Upon reflection of where you might end up in life, you must begin to realize that a lot of the outcome has to do with whom you are affiliated with. People can help us, but at times they can also hinder our progress. You can't be moved by what other people think or say about you. Instead you must develop your self-esteem enabling you to rise above it all. For the most part another person's opinion is only that, an opinion and has no bearing on whom you are as a person. I am not saying that you should not listen to the opinions of those with whom you come in contact. I am saying to be cautious with whom you allow to program your thoughts.

Just because someone has something to say does not mean that it is the right answer for you at that time. It is okay to get constructive criticism. But you do not have to follow another person's advice, because it may not always be good advice. You will have to make a choice to either listen to the advice, continue in the direction you are headed and learn as you go. We all have choices. The key to life is making the best choices we can. Then make the best out of the choices you have made. Life has a habit of giving you another chance to improve your situation. So glean what you are supposed to learn and move on.

You can change your destiny at anytime, simply by taking control of your life and associating with groups of people who are going in the direction you would like to end at. Whatever it takes, no matter where you are, put yourself in an environment that promotes growth. You must pick people who will mentor you. The more successful the people are the bigger they will be. And the reason you want to look for bigger people is because big people will not be intimidated by whatever you have decided to accomplish. They will cheer you on and do whatever they can to help inspire you to make your dream a reality. The bottom line is they will believe in you and help you to work more diligently toward your ultimate objectives. That is why it is so important to get with people who are going in the same direction that you want to travel.

How you live your life will have an effect on the people you come in contact with, especially children. Their minds are like sponges. They will imitate whatever they see you do. The adage of, "do what I tell you to do," is out the window. Your actions speak so loud they can not hear what you say. If you want the best results from our future leaders, you must model that example. When children or young adults see a model of how a situation should be handled they tend to gravitate toward that example. When I was younger, I had teachers that were so nice and kind, who showed a sincere desire to see me grow and develop into a responsible individual. Because of their love and concern, I didn't want to disappoint them.

Please make the assumption that children want to act right, that they want to succeed and you will find a pleasant surprise. Most children will be drawn into your web of expectations. They will fulfill their obligation, because they want to please you since you took the time to believe in them and help them to nurture their gifts and talents. And be aware of the example you follow, because it can and will have a devastating effect on what your future prospects will be.

When we are young we have our parents always there to tell us what we should or should not do. They are in our mix, telling us we shouldn't hang out with this person or that person. At the time we don't want to hear it because we think they just want to interfere with our joy and don't want us to have any fun in life. More times than not, if we go and research the background of some of the people we connected ourselves with, we will likely find that whatever troubles they got themselves into may have had a lot to do with the people that they were associating with at the time. Being involved with the wrong people can hinder you. If our parents were right we should go back and let them know that their advice was dead on and we appreciate their words of wisdom.

In the process of reading this book I hope you have discovered that you have talents that will lead you onto greatness. Remember to lean on your inner signals. Outside stimulation is good and it has its place because seeing others achieve can and should inspire you to continue on down the path you have chosen for success. But true greatness only comes when one follows their own inner signals. The inner signal represents the true essence of whom you are and who you are truly capable of becoming. So when you get hunches and inspirations do not always cast them aside or put them on the back burner. These are probably the spark that is waiting to be ignited to cause the internal combustion that will propel you to the top of your desired field of choice.

Within each of us we have the capacity and ability to achieve greatness. What we must do is hone our skills and talents to steer us in the direction that would be most suitable for our specific personalities. We definitely want to find something that lines up with who we are. For instance, if you know that you are an introverted person, I do not foresee you pursuing a career as a public speaker or stand up comedian. On the other hand if you are outgoing and have a bubbly personality, your talents would not be best served as a mortician.

We must study ourselves and then line up with what best suits us. There is something out there that fits each of us. We must try it on for size. Life is full of all types of success stories that come out of places or things that you would never have looked into. Take for example the paper clip. How were papers held together before it? Or the innovative idea of a sticky note pad. Write a reminder, peel it off, and then stick it anywhere. The list could go on and on. The basic premise of these items is that they came from the idea of helping to make someone else's life a little less complicated.

I know that there is something inside you just waiting to come out, letting the world know that you have a better mousetrap. So come on and share your experiences with us. We are interested in what you have to offer. The fear will go away if you will take the first steps toward reaching your goal. With each step that you take forward, you will gain more confidence and it will become easier and easier to take the rest. So get a purpose, a smile, and get on with life!

Endnotes

1. Proverbs 23: 7 , The Holy Bible King James Version (KJV), originally published in 1611
2. Psycho-Cybernetics, Dr. Maxwell Maltz, 2006
3. Napoleon Hill, Think and Grow Rich, 1937
4. I John 4:18 (KJV)
5. Wikipedia, "Oprah Winfrey," [Internet – WWW, URL], http://en.wikipedia.org/wiki/Oprah_Winfrey
6. I Corinthians 14:33 (KJV)
7. Matthew 12:34 (KJV)
8. Philippians 4:19 (KJV)
9. Philippians 4:13 (KJV)
10. Matthew 11:28-29 (KJV)
11. Proverbs 18:21 (KJV)
12. Mark 11:24 (KJV)
13. Proverbs 3:5 (KJV)
14. Dr. Wayne Dyer, The Sky is the Limit, 1980
15. Hebrews 11:1 (KJV)
16. Mark 11:23 (KJV)
17. Ecclesiastes 1:9 (KJV)
18. Galatians 6:7 (KJV)
19. John F. Kennedy, Inaugural Speech, Washington DC, January 20, 1961
20. GQ Magazine 1998
21. Wikipedia, "Muhammad Ali," [Internet – WWW, URL], http://www.en.wikipedia.org/wiki/Muhammad_Ali
22. Proverbs 8:12 (KJV)

23. John 16:33 (KJV)
24. I Corinthians 15:58 (KJV)
25. John 10:10 (KJV)
26. James 4:7 (KJV)
27. 2 Corinthians 1:20 (KJV)
28. Act 10:34 (KJV)
29. Ecclesiastes 9:11 (KJV)
30. Hamlet, Act 1, Scene 3, line 84
31. Philippians 4:19 (KJV)
32. Revelation 3:20 (KJV)
33. Psalm 23:6 (KJV)
34. Proverbs 9:10 (KJV)
35. I John 2:27 (KJV)
36. Abraham Lincoln Online, Education Links, Abraham Lincoln, [Internet – WWW, URL], http://www.showcase.netins.net/web/creative/Lincoln/education/failures.htm
37. James 1:5 (KJV)
38. Wikipedia, "Joseph P. Kennedy," [Internet – WWW,URL], http://www.en.wikipedia.org/Joseph Kennedy
39. Proverbs 29:18 (KJV)
40. Wikipedia, "Ben Sweetland," [Internet – WWW, URL], http://www.en.wikipedia.org/Ben_Sweetland
41. Isaiah 59:19 (KJV)
42. Malachi 3:10 (KJV)
43. Luke 6:38 (KJV)
44. Job 13:15 (KJV)
45. Proverbs 18:24 (KJV)
46. Wikipedia, "Franklin D. Roosevelt" [Internet – WWW, URL], http://www.en.wikipedia.org/Franklin_Roosevelt, President of USA 1933-1945
47. Philippians 2:10-11 (KJV)
48. Brad Herzog, The Sports 100: The One Hundred Most Important People in American Sports History New York: Simon & Schuster, 1995
49. Psalms 91:1 (KJV)
50. Hebrews 11:6 (KJV)
51. John 4:24 (KJV)

References

Author Unknown, "Ronald Reagan," People Magazine, June 21, 2004

Author Unknown, "Irma Elder," Corps Michigan Edition Magazine, March 2002

The Elder Automotive Group, "About Us," [Internet – WWW, URL], http://www.elderautomotivegroup.com/content_meet.htm

Enterprising Woman, "Elder," [Internet – WWW, URL; http://www.enterprisingwomen.com/elder.htm

Printed in the United States
97745LV00003B/346-351/A

9 781604 771138